ENGLISH G

LIGHTHOUSE

Englisch für DaZ-Lernende

1|2

ONLINE-Angebot

mit Audios und Lösungen online

Cornelsen

1 Welcome to our class

Good morning.

Welcome to our class.

Nice to meet you.

My name is Mr Chan.

I'm your English teacher.

classmate

Hello.

Hi.

What's your name?

I'm Jill.

Are you a student too?

No, I'm not.

Where are you from?

I'm from Syria.

My poster is about Syria.

How old are you?

I'm 13 years old.

What's your favourite music?

My favourite music is hip-hop.

Rap and hip-hop are OK.

But my favourite music is house.

There's a green door.

There are lockers.

school

Let's go.

→ My Words, pp. 14–15

1 Welcome to our class

12 twelve
13 thirteen
14 fourteen
20 twenty

a 1 Look at page 4. Listen and read.
b Read the texts. Match the pictures to the texts.

I'm Jill. I'm 20 years old. I'm from England.	My name is Yero. I'm 12 years old. I'm from Guinea.	I'm Olga. I'm 14 years old. I'm from Russia.	My name is Mo. I'm 13 years old. I'm from Syria.

2 What about you?

a Write about yourself:
- What's your name?
- How old are you?
- Where are you from?

b Ask and answer the questions with a partner.

your picture

I'm ____________
____
____

TIP: Change the green words in the sentences from 1b:
I'm Jill.
→ *I'm Adnan.*

3 Your classmates

a Look and read.
b Write about a student from your class and draw a picture.

This is Jill.
She's 20.
She's from England.
She's a language assistant.

This is Mo.
He's 13.
He's from Syria.
He's a student.

She is a student.

He is 12.

TIP: Change the green words in the sentences:
This is Yero.
→ *This is Jasmin.*

4 Act out the dialogue

a 1 Listen to and read the dialogue on page 4 again.
b Act out the dialogue in a group. Or record it.

→ My Words, pp. 14–15

1 Welcome to our class

1 Personal pronouns

2 Listen and read. Listen again and repeat.

I · you · he · she · it

we · you · they

2 The verb *be* in the present tense: positive statements

a 3 Listen and read. Listen again and repeat.

I'm from England. I am …	You're from Syria. You are …	He's … He is …	She's … She is …	It's … It is …
We're … We are …	You're … You are …	They're … They are …		

b 4 Listen and read.

c Act out the dialogue from 2b in a group. Make your own dialogues.

Afghanistan • Croatia • Denmark • Eritrea • France • Germany • Georgia • Iran • Iraq • Italy • Lebanon • Nigeria • Portugal • Russia • Serbia • Somalia • Spain • Sweden • Turkey • the USA • …

d Complete the sentences.

He (2 x) • She • It • We • They	+	's (is) • 're (are)

1 This is Yero. *He's* from Guinea.

2 This is Olga and this is Yero. ________ in my class.

3 Olga and I are friends. ________ in the classroom.

4 This is Jill. ________ from England.

5 This is Mr Chan. ________ my English teacher.

6 This is my favourite poster. ________ about Syria.

3 The verb *be* in the present tense: negative statements

5 Listen and read. Listen again and repeat.

I'm not 15. I am not 15.	You're not … You are not …	He isn't … He is not …	She isn't … She is not …	It isn't … It is not …
We aren't … We are not …	You aren't … You are not …	They aren't … They are not …		

4 The verb *be* in the present tense: questions and short answers

a Read the boxes.

Am I 14? Are you …? Is he/she/it …? Are we …? Are you …? Are they …?	Yes,	I am. you are. he/she/it is. we are. you are. they are.	No,	I'm not. you aren't. he/she/it isn't. we aren't. you aren't. they aren't.	**Questions with question words:** What's (=is) your name? Where are you from? → Module 3, p. 33 (questions)

b 6 Listen. Then write six or more questions in your exercise book. Answer the questions.

Are you Is Jill Is Yero	from England • from Russia • 12 years old • Mo's classmate • a student • a teacher • …?

Are you from England? – No, I'm not.

b Ask and answer your questions with a partner.

Numbers:
0 zero, oh
1 one
2 two
3 three
4 four
5 five
6 six
7 seven
8 eight
9 nine
10 ten
11 eleven
12 twelve
13 thirteen
14 fourteen
15 fifteen
16 sixteen
17 seventeen
18 eighteen
19 nineteen
20 twenty

What's your telephone number?

You write	You say
0	oh
00	double oh
99	double nine

→ Numbers, p. 111
→ My Words, pp. 14–15

1 Numbers

a Listen to and read the numbers in the margin.
b Listen and write down the telephone numbers.

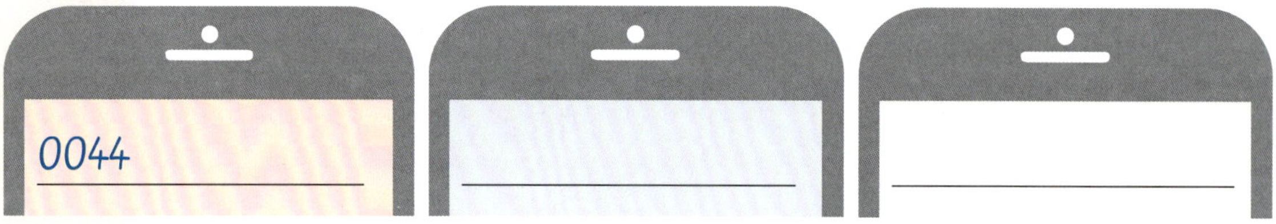

c Write down two numbers or telephone numbers. Ask and answer with a partner. Write down and check your partner's numbers.

Me: ______________________
____

My partner: ______________________
____

d Complete the crossword puzzle.

1 one, ..., five, seven
2 ..., four, six, eight
3 zero, six, twelve, ...
4 five, eight, ..., fourteen
5 eleven, nine, seven, ...
6 eight, eleven, fourteen, ...

2 Thinking about languages

a Write and say the numbers 1–10 in your language(s).
b Talk to your classmates and find out about other languages.

	English	Arabic	Fula	Russian	...
1	one	واحد	goo	один	...
2	two	اثنان	zizi	два	

3 Colours

a 🔊9 📖 Listen to and read the colour words in the margin.

b 🔊10 ✎ Listen and colour the pens.

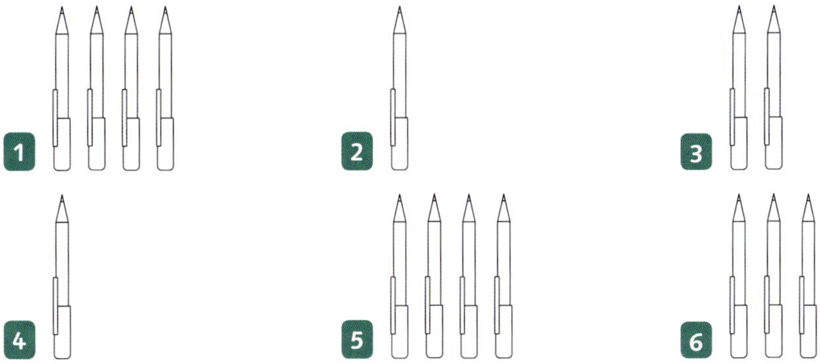

c 📖 ✎ Find the colour words and mark them.

N	C	O	H	B	O	G	R	E	Y
A	R	A	L	L	V	D	Y	O	K
C	Y	L	P	U	R	P	L	E	Y
R	E	D	I	E	B	L	A	C	K
H	L	E	N	G	R	E	E	N	A
H	L	L	K	U	O	W	T	E	N
D	O	L	L	G	W	H	I	T	E
H	W	O	R	A	N	G	E	R	P

black • blue • brown • green • ~~grey~~ • orange • pink • purple • red • white • yellow

d 🔊11 ✎ Listen and colour the things.

1 a chair
2 a clock
3 a cupboard
4 a door
5 a poster
6 a smartboard
7 a table
8 a tablet
9 a window

e 🔊11 ✎ Listen again and write sentences 1–9 in your exercise book.

1. The chair is ...

Colours:
black
blue
brown
green
grey
orange
pink
purple
red
white
yellow

Things in the classroom:
chair
clock
cupboard
door
smartboard
table
tablet
window

English and German

The door is red.
Die Tür ist rot.

The chair is blue.
Der Stuhl ist blau

The smartboard is black.
Das Smartboard ist schwarz.

→ My Words, pp. 14–15

Short and long forms
short: There**'s** a table.
long: There **is** a table.

Singular and plural
There**'s** (= **is**) a table.
There **are** books.

book
pen

singular **plural**

singular	plural
one pen	two pen**s**
chair	chair**s**
book	book**s**
table	table**s**
glass	glass**es**

the plural: noun + **s**

new ↔ old
full ↔ empty
glass

***a* or *an*?**
Check how you say the next word:
a red chair
a full glass
a tablet
an orange chair
an empty glass

With **A, E, I, O, U** you say **an**.

→ Sounds, p. 110

⊞
There's a book.
There are books.
⊟
There isn't a book.
There aren't any books.

→ My Words, pp. 14–15

4 There are two orange chairs

a 12 Listen and read.

There's a smartboard.
There's a white table.
There are two orange chairs.
There are five books.
There are …

books • chairs • a clock •
a door • pens • a table • tablets

b 12 Listen again and look. Write in your exercise book:

There's …	*There are …*
There's a smartboard.	*There are two orange chairs.*

5 When to say *a* or *an*

a 13 Listen and read. Listen again and repeat.

a grey chair

an orange chair

a full glass

an empty glass

a new book

an old book

b Write *a* or *an*.

1 There's _____ old clock.
2 There's _____ new smartboard.
3 There's _____ yellow table.
4 There's _____ empty locker.

c Practise a and b. Read aloud and record it.

6 There aren't any empty glasses

a Look and read. Read aloud.

There isn't an orange table.
There's a red table.
There aren't any empty glasses.
There are full glasses.
There aren't any new books.
There are old books.

b Write six or more sentences about your school in your exercise book.

There's There isn't There are There aren't any	English dictionaries • lockers • new chairs • nice students • nice teachers • a cupboard • a smartboard • …	in my classroom. at my school.

There aren't any lockers at my school …

in my classroom
at my school
a nice student / teacher

Singular and plural
one dictionary
two dictionaries
y → ies

7 Is there a smartboard?

a 14 Listen and read.

Mr Chan: Well, Yero. Let's see …
What's in our new classroom?
Is there a smartboard?
Yero: Yes, there is, Mr Chan.
Mr Chan: Are there any tablets?
Yero: Yes, there are.
Mr Chan: Are there any dictionaries?
Yero: No, there aren't.

Is there a smartboard?
Yes, there is.
No, there isn't.

Are there any dictionaries?
Yes, there are.
No, there aren't.

b Mark the questions and the answers.
c Write six or more questions about your school in your exercise book.

Is there a/an Are there any	canteen • English dictionary • library • red pens • students • swimming pool • nice teachers • …	in our classroom? at our school?

TIP: Look up words in an online dictionary or in the English-German dictionary for this workbook.

d Ask a partner and write down your partner's answers.
e Record your questions and answers.

8 Thinking about languages

a Look and read.

friend

parent

teacher

friend
parents *(pl)*

b How do you say 'hello' to friends, parents and teachers in your language(s)? Talk to your classmates.

→ My Words, pp. 14–15

TIP: There is a word list **My Words** at the end of each **Module**.

1 Learning words

a Read. Then look at the word list *My Words* on pages 14–15.

English	German	My notes
Nice to meet you.	Schön, dich/Sie kennen zu lernen.	
Welcome to our class.	Willkommen in unserer Klasse.	
Hello. Hi.	Hallo. Hi.	

TIP: Add to **My notes**:
- words in your or other languages
- English examples
- pictures

b Add to the word list on pages 14–15:

1. Write words in your language or other languages.
2. Write English examples.
3. Draw pictures.

English	My notes
Hello. Hi.	Хей! مرحبا
Nice to meet you.	*Meet your classmates.*
table	*a table ↔ a tablet* 

TIP:
1. Practise 5–10 minutes every day.
2. Practise 7–10 new words every day.
3. Repeat the words.
4. Practise with other students.

c Practise your words every day.

2 Find your way of learning

Read the tips and try them out:

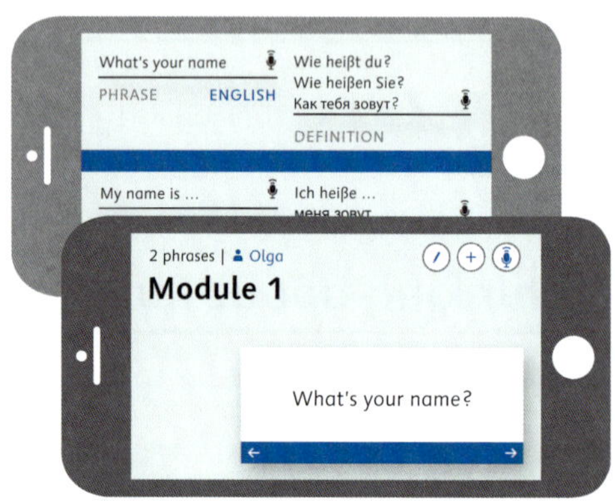

1. Write difficult words and phrases on notes and put them up.

2. Make vocabulary cards with a vocabulary app:
   - Write the new words and phrases.
   - Write the words and phrases in German and your language(s).
   - You can add pictures.
   - Practise on your smartphone.

TIP: You can copy words and phrases from the English-German dictionary into the vocabulary app.

1 Mark the words with the right colours.

◯ blue ◯ brown ◯ green ◯ orange
◯ purple ◯ yellow ◯ grey ◯ black
◯ red ◯ pink ◯ white

2 15 Listen and mark the right numbers.

1

1	2	3	4	5
6	7	8	9	10
11	12	13	14	15

2

2	4	6	8	10
12	14	16	18	20
10	0	1	5	7

3

3	5	8	1	15
11	13	6	2	4
7	14	18	9	6

3 Write about yourself.

- What's your name?
- How old are you? ______________________
- What's your favourite music? ______________________
- Are you a teacher? ______________________

____

4 Look at the pictures. Complete the sentences.

1 ______________________ a blue table.
2 ______________________ a green chair.
3 ______________________ empty glasses.
4 ______________________ full glasses.

5 Tick the right answers.

1 Are you a student?

▢ No, I'm not. ▢ Yes, you are. ▢ Yes, I am. ▢ Yes, he is.

2 Is your English teacher from Germany?

▢ No, she isn't. ▢ No, he isn't. ▢ Yes, he is. ▢ Yes, she is.

3 Is there a smartboard in your classroom?

▢ Yes, there are. ▢ No, there aren't. ▢ Yes, there is. ▢ No, there isn't.

1 Welcome to our class

English	German	My notes
Nice to meet you.	Schön, dich/Sie kennen zu lernen.	
Welcome to our class.	Willkommen in unserer Klasse.	
Hello. Hi.	Hallo. Hi.	
Good morning.	Guten Morgen.	
What's your name?	Wie heißt du?/ Wie heißen Sie?	
My name is Mr Chan. **I'm** your English teacher.	Ich heiße Herr Chan. Ich bin dein/euer Englischlehrer.	
How old are you?	Wie alt bist du?/ Wie alt sind Sie?	
I'm 13 (years old).	Ich bin 13 (Jahre alt).	
Where are you from?	Woher kommst du?/ Woher kommen Sie?	
I'm from Syria.	Ich komme aus Syrien.	
My poster is about Syria.	Mein Poster zeigt Syrien.	
What's your favourite music?	Was ist deine/Ihre Lieblingsmusik?	
My favourite music is hip-hop.	Meine Lieblingsmusik ist Rap.	
Rap and hip-hop are **OK**. **But** my favourite music is ...	Rap und Hip-Hop sind okay. Aber meine Lieblingsmusik ist ...	
There's (= **there is**) a door. **There are** lockers.	Es gibt eine Tür. / Da ist ... Es gibt Schließfächer.	
Are you a student too?	Bist du auch ein/e Schüler/in? / Sind Sie ...?	
Are you from England? Yes, I am. / No, I'm not. Yes, we are. / No, we aren't.	Bist du aus England?/ Seid ihr ...? / Sind Sie ...? Ja. / Nein.	
at my school **in** my classroom	in/an meiner Schule in meinem Klassenzimmer	
Let's go.	Lass(t) uns gehen.	

English	German	My notes
Colours (Farben) ● **black** schwarz ● **blue** blau ● **brown** braun ● **green** grün ● **grey** grau ● **orange** orange ● **pink** rosa, pink ● **purple** lila ● **red** rot ○ **white** weiß ● **yellow** gelb		
There isn't a blue chair. **There aren't any** red chairs.	Es gibt keinen blauen Stuhl. Es gibt keine roten Stühle.	
What's your (telephone) number?	Wie ist deine Nummer?	
The numbers from 0 to 20 (Die Zahlen von 0 bis 20) 0 zero, 1 one, 2 two, 3 three, 4 four, 5 five, 6 six, 7 seven, 8 eight, 9 nine, 10 ten, 11 eleven, 12 twelve, 13 thirteen, 14 fourteen, 15 fifteen, 16 sixteen, 17 seventeen, 18 eighteen, 19 nineteen, 20 twenty → Numbers, p. 109		
People:	**Personen:**	
teacher	der Lehrer / die Lehrerin	
classmate	der Mitschüler / die Mitschülerin	
student	der Schüler / die Schülerin	
friend	der Freund / die Freundin	
parents *(pl)*	die Eltern *(Pl.)*	
Things in the classroom:	**Dinge im Klassenzimmer:**	
pen	der Kugelschreiber, der Stift	
chair	der Stuhl	
clock	die Uhr	
cupboard	der Schrank	
smartboard	das Smartboard	
table	der Tisch	
tablet	das Tablet	
window	das Fenster	
an **old** book a **new** book	ein altes Buch ein neues Buch	
a **full** glass an **empty** glass	ein volles Glas ein leeres Glas	
dictionary, *pl* dictionaries	das Wörterbuch	

2 My school week

It's 8 o'clock.

It's Tuesday.

What do we do every Tuesday?

I teach English every Tuesday.

(to) teach English

(to) learn English

(to) go to the computer room

(to) take a test

sometimes

Look at the timetable, please.

I like PE too.

I don't like history.

Subjects:
English
maths
PE
history

Open your books at page 42.

Can you read task 1, please?

(to) play football

(to) study English

(to) do homework

after school
on Wednesdays
at the weekend

always
never
usually
every day

→ My Words, pp. 28–29

1 Every Tuesday

a 🔊16 Look at page 16. Listen and read.
b Read aloud.

2 Right or wrong?

a Tick the right answers. Check your answers on page 16.

☐ It's 10 o'clock.
☑ It's Tuesday.
☐ The students open their books.
☐ They go to the computer room.
☐ Yero studies English at the weekend.
☐ Mr Chan teaches English.

b Match the sentence parts. Check your answers on page 16.

1 Yero — D
2 Mo
3 Mr Chan
4 Olga

A teaches English.
B goes to the gym every day.
C likes history.
D plays football.

3 School things

a 🔊17 Look at the pictures. Listen and repeat.

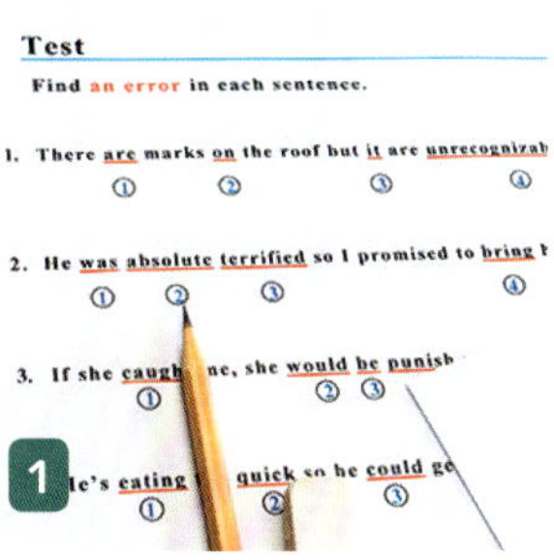

1

2

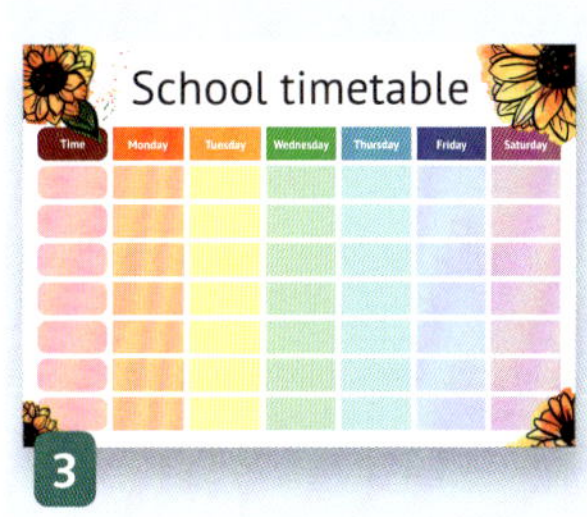

3

4

5

6

b Look at the pictures again. Number the words (1–6).

☐ a timetable
(1) a test
☐ a computer
☐ a pencil
☐ an exercise book
☐ a pen

TIP: You can read or act out the dialogue with your classmates. One classmate is Mo, one classmate is Jill, etc.

TIP:
1. Read the sentences.
2. Read or listen to the text again.
3. Tick or match the sentences.
4. Check your answers.

School things:
computer
exercise book
pen
pencil
test
timetable

TIP: Label the things in your classroom. Add more labels every day. Do the same at home.

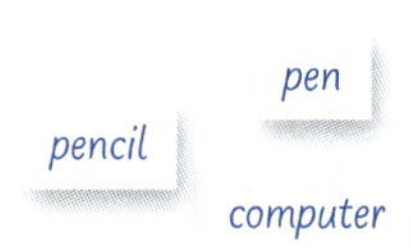

Look up new words in an online dictionary.

→ p. 26 (Online dictionaries and apps)

→ My Words, pp. 28–29

1 The simple present: positive statements

a Read the boxes.

I You We You They	learn English.
He/She/It	learns English.

The simple present has one form for *I*, *you*, *we* and *they*. For he, she, it you add an -s.

I go to the gym every day.
Mr Chan teaches English every Tuesday.
The class sometimes takes a test.
Mo never studies at the weekend.

You use the simple present to say what you usually do or what usually happens.
Signal words: every day, on Wednesdays, always, sometimes, usually, never, …

b Complete the sentences with *learn or learns*.

1 They learn English every day.
2 He never ________ English at the weekend.
3 We ________ English every Tuesday.
4 You always ________ English at the weekend.
5 She ________ English on Wednesdays.
6 I sometimes ________ English with my friend.

c Mark the signal words in sentences 1–6.

2 The simple present: special verbs

a Read the box.

⚠ Be careful with the spelling of these verbs:
teach: he/she/it teaches
go, do: he/she/it goes, does
study: he/she/it studies
have: he/she/it has

be: I am
we/you/they are
he/she/it is

→ Module 1, p. 6 (be)

b 18 Complete the sentences. Listen and check.

1 Mr Chan ________ **(teach)** English every Tuesday.
2 The students ________ **(look)** at the timetable every day.
3 Mo never ________ **(study)** at the weekend.
4 Olga ________ **(go)** to the gym every day.
5 They sometimes ________ **(take)** a test on Tuesdays.
6 Olga ________ **(have)** two favourite subjects: English and maths.
7 Mo ________ **(do)** his homework after school.

3 The simple present: negative statements

a Read the boxes. Then mark *doesn't* or *don't* in the sentences.

I You We You They	don't study.
He/She/It	doesn't study.

In negative statements in the simple present you use don't for *I*, *you*, *we*, *they*. You use doesn't for he, she, it.

After don't and doesn't you use the infinitive of the verb:
⊞ Mr Chan teaches English.
⊟ Mr Chan doesn't teach history.

1 Mr Chan and Mrs Kern **doesn't/don't** teach on Sundays.
2 Mo **doesn't/don't** study at the weekend.
3 Jill **doesn't/don't** go to school.
4 We **doesn't/don't** have PE on Fridays.
5 I **doesn't/don't** like school.
6 Olga **doesn't/don't** play football.

4 *Can* and *can't (cannot)*

a Read the boxes. Then complete the sentences with *can* or *can't*.

Positive statements

I/You He/She/It We/You/They	can play.

Negative statements

I/You He/She/It We/You/They	can't (= cannot) play.

1

2

3

4

1 He __________ go to school.
2 She __________ play football.
3 He __________ do his homework.
4 She __________ open the door.

b 19 Listen and check.
c What can or can't you do? Write four or more sentences.

I can I can't	do my homework after school • go to the gym on Mondays • play football/ basketball/... • read an English book • study at the weekend • ...

I can't play football. I can ...

d Compare your sentences with a partner.

School starts at 8 o'clock.
(to) wear your own clothes
(to) wear a school uniform
(to) get a mark

1 Schools in Britain and Germany

a 20 Look and read. Then listen to Jill.

b 20 Listen again. Write *G* for Germany and *B* for Britain.

1

2

3

4

1 Students wear school uniforms. B
2 School starts at 8 o'clock. ☐
3 Students get marks A–F. ☐
4 Students wear their own clothes. ☐
5 School starts at 8:45. ☐
6 Students get marks 1–6. ☐

5

6
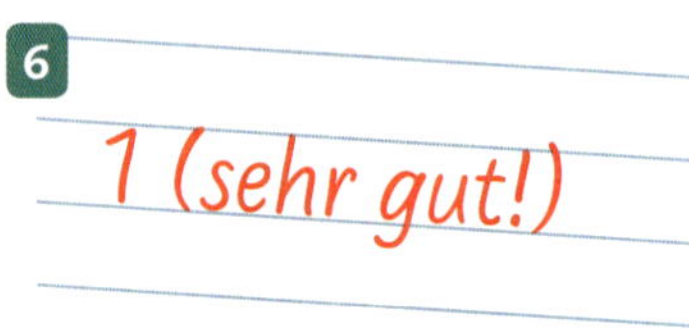

School finishes at 3:15.
(to) speak English/German

2 What can you say about your school in Germany?

a Write six or more sentences in your exercise book.

At our school we (don't)	have a computer room • wear a school uniform/our own clothes • get marks 1–6 • speak English/German with our friends • take tests every week • …

Our school	starts at 8:00 • usually finishes at 3:15 • is great/OK/nice • …

At our school we get marks 1–6. We don't …

TIP: You can look up more words in a dictionary.
→ p. 26 (How to use a dictionary)

→ My Words, pp. 28–29

b Compare your sentences with a partner.

3 Thinking about cultures

a What do you know about schools in other countries? Write down ideas.

In Guinea school usually starts at ...
Students usually wear ...

b Talk to your classmates.
c Make a poster about schools in one country. Present it to the class.

TIP: You can use words and sentences from page 20. You can look up more words in a dictionary.

→ p. 26 (How to use a dictionary)

4 The days of the week

a 21 Listen to and read the days of the week in the margin.
b 21 Listen again and repeat.

Days of the week:
Monday
Tuesday
Wednesday
Thursday
Friday
Saturday
Sunday

5 Mo's week

22 Listen to Mo. Write the days into the puzzle. Then complete Mo's speech bubble.

1 Mo does his English homework on ... .
2 He studies with his friend on ... .
3 He goes to school at 9:50 on ... .
4 He goes to the gym on ... .
5 He has English and German on ... .
6 He can use his brother's computer on ... .

(to) use a computer

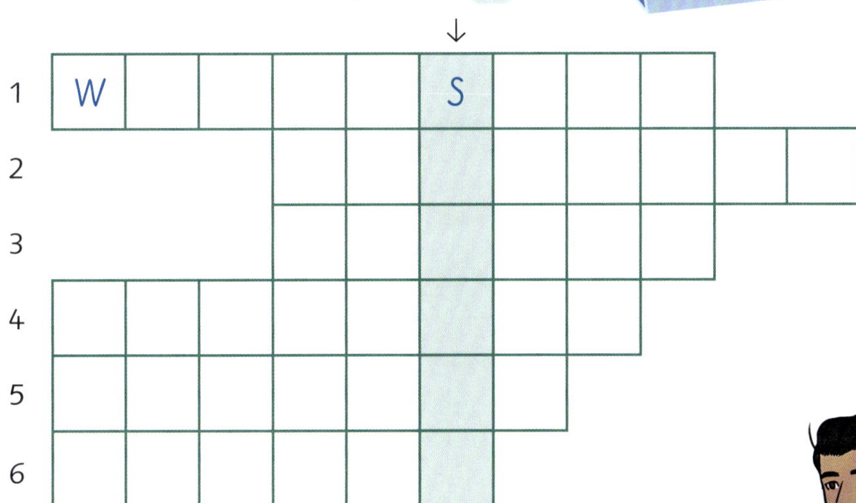

→ My Words, pp. 28–29

Numbers:
20 twenty
21 twenty-one
22 twenty-two
23 twenty-three
24 twenty-four
25 twenty-five
26 twenty-six
27 twenty-seven
28 twenty-eight
29 twenty-nine
30 thirty
31 thirty-one
...

It's the same for 40, 50, 60, 70, 80 and 90.

40 forty	70 seventy
50 fifty	80 eighty
60 sixty	90 ninety

→ Numbers, p. 111

6 Numbers from 20 to 99

a 23 Listen to and read the numbers in the margin.
b 23 Listen again and repeat.
c Match the numbers to the words.

86 · 70 · 34 · 53 · 91

forty-five
thirty-four
thirty-three
seventy
ninety-nine
eighty-six
forty-seven
ninety-one
fifty-three
sixty-eight

33 · 99 · 45 · 47 · 68

d 24 Listen and write the numbers in words.

~~27~~ • 45 • 55 • 78 • 86 • 92

1 *twenty-seven* ______
2 ______
3 ______
4 ______
5 ______
6 ______

7 What's the time?

a 25 Listen and repeat.

b 25 Listen again and complete the sentences.

1 It's *eight* o'clock.
2 It's ten past ______.
3 It's quarter past ______.
4 It's ______ past ______.
5 It's half past ______.
6 It's quarter to ______.
7 It's ______ to one.
8 It's ______ to ______.

What's the time?
It's ...

ten o'clock

ten fifteen
quarter past ten

ten thirty
half past ten

ten forty-five
quarter to eleven

ten fifty-five
five to eleven

ten oh five
five past ten

→ My Words, pp. 28–29

8 A timetable

a 26 Look at the timetable and listen.
What are Jill's favourite subjects? Tick.

- ☐ PE
- ☐ science
- ☐ ICT
- ☐ art

Lesson/ Time		Mon	Tue	Wed	Thu	Fri
	8.45–9.00			Assembly		
1	9.00–10.00	PE	English	Art	English	Maths
2	10.00–11.00	PE	English	English	Geography	ICT
	11.00–11.20			Break		
3	11.20–12.20	Science	Music	Science	History	German

School subjects:
art
English
German
geography
history
ICT
music
maths
PE
science

lesson
break

b Look at the timetable again. Tick the right answers.

- ☐ School starts at 8:45.
- ☐ Lesson 1 on Monday is maths.
- ☐ The class takes a break at 10:15.
- ☐ Lesson 3 on Wednesday is science.
- ☐ There are no art lessons.
- ☐ Lessons 1 and 2 on Tuesday are English.

c Complete the sentences.

1 PE ______ is from 9 to 11 o'clock on Monday.

2 ______ is at 9 o'clock on Friday.

3 ______ is at 11:20 on Monday and Wednesday.

4 ______ is at 10 o'clock on Thursday.

from 9 to 11 o'clock

d Write your timetable in English. Talk to a partner about your timetable. You can use sentences from b and c.

→ My Words, pp. 28–29

Listen, please.
Read page 32.

English and German
Listen, please.
Hör bitte zu!
Hört bitte zu!
Hören Sie bitte zu!

→ Classroom English, p. 112

9 Classroom talk

27 What do you hear? Listen, read and tick.

1 ◯ Open your books at page 3. ◯ Open your tablets, please.
2 ◯ The lesson starts at 12:20. ◯ The lesson finishes at 12:20.
3 ◯ Read page 32 in your science book. ◯ Read page 32 in your history book.
4 ◯ Look at the timetable. ◯ Look at page 99.
5 ◯ Look, please. ◯ Listen, please.

Can you spell that word, please?

The alphabet:
Aa Bb Cc Dd Ed Ff Gg
Hh Ii Jj Kk Ll Mm Nn
Oo Pp Qq Rr Ss Tt Uu
Vv Ww Xx Yy Zz

→ Alphabet, p. 110

10 Can you spell that word, please?

a 28 Listen to and read the alphabet in the margin.
b 29 Listen to and read the alphabet in sound groups. Repeat.

A H J K   B C D E G P T V   I Y
Q U W   F L M N S X Z   O   R

c 30 Listen and write down the words.

1 *p* _ _ _ _ _ _   2 _ _ _ _ _ _   3 _ _ _ _ _ _ _ _   4 _ _ _ _ _ _

d 31 Spell the words. Then listen and check.

1 favourite
2 uniform
3 classroom
4 lesson
5 science
6 school

You write	You say
ss	double s
oo	double oh

English and German
I **can** **read** this text.
Ich **kann** diesen Text **lesen**.

11 Can a teacher wear a school uniform?

Write correct sentences with *can* and *can't*.

1 geography. | teach | can't | ~~A maths teacher~~
A maths teacher
____

2 can't | The students | go | on a Sunday. | to school
____

3 English | after school. | can | They | study
____

4 wear | A teacher | can't | a school uniform.
____

→ My Words, pp. 28–29

12 Write about your school week

There's a new student in your class.
Write a letter or make a video blog.
Tell the student about:

- your class and classroom
- your school week
- your favourite subjects
- your teachers
- what you and your classmates do after school

TIP: Change the green words in the text:
Our classroom is nice.
→ *Our classroom is OK.*

Welcome to our class, Bilal!

Our class

In our class we have twenty-one students.
Our classroom is nice.
We have a smartboard and a computer.
But we don't have tablets.

→ Numbers, p. 111

→ Module 1, p. 15 (things in the classroom)

new • OK • old • …

English dictionaries • new tables • …

Our school week

School usually starts at 7:40.
We have two breaks in the morning, at 9:30 and at 11:20.
School usually finishes at 3:15.
On Fridays it finishes at 2:30.

→ p. 22 (time)

We go to the computer room on Tuesdays and Fridays. We often watch videos.
And we sometimes make videos.

→ p. 21 (days)

Monday • Tuesday • …

take tests • listen to music • make posters • act out dialogues • …

My favourite subject is PE.
I like geography too.
What are your favourite subjects?

→ p. 23 (subjects)

art • history • ICT • …

Our teachers

Mr Kienbaum teaches English.
Mrs Weiler teaches German and maths.

After school

Our class is really nice. After school we sometimes meet in the school garden and study. You can come with us!

do homework • study English/German/… • meet in the school canteen/cafe/… • play football • …

Your classmate
Miriam

TIP: You can look up more words in an online dictionary.
→ p. 26 (Online dictionaries and apps)

> **TIP:** There's an online English-German dictionary for this workbook.

1 How to use a dictionary

a Read the example from an English-German dictionary.

> The words are in alphabetical order: A, B, C, D, … The A-words (B-words, …) are in alphabetical order too: after, always, answer, …

C

class [kla:s] *n* (Schul-)Klasse

classmate ['kla:smeɪt] *n* Mitschüler/in, Klassenkamerad/in

classroom ['kla:sru:m] *n* Klassenzimmer

> This is how you pronounce (say) the word.

> **n (noun):** a thing, a person or a concept
> **v (verb):** you can do it or it happens

→ Alphabet, p. 110

b Write these words in alphabetical order.

clothes • test • computer • pen

1 ________ **2** ________ **3** ________ **4** ________

c Find these words in a dictionary. Write *n* (noun) or *v* (verb).

playground	n	training		invitation	
celebrate		look *sth.* up		meet	

2 Online dictionaries and apps

a Look at the online dictionary and read the boxes.

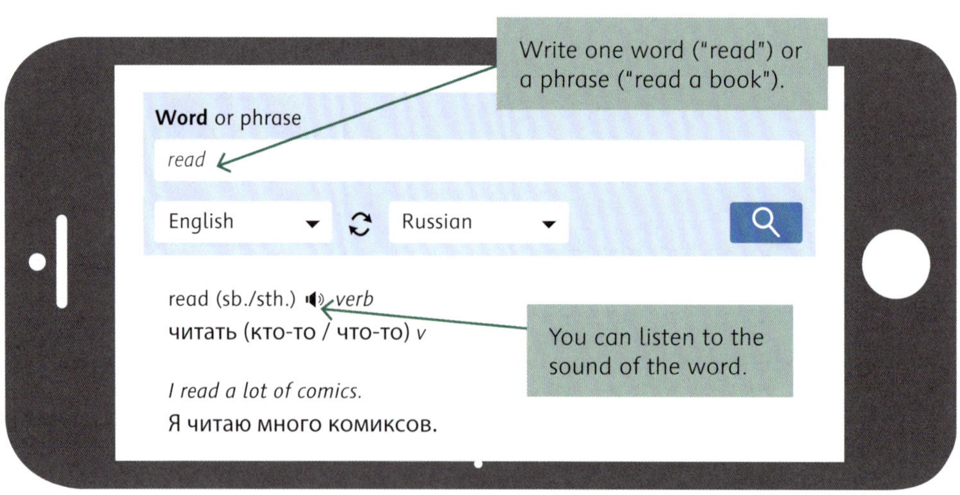

> **TIP:** There are lots of free online dictionaries and apps.

b Look up the verb *read* in an online dictionary. Write down the meaning in German and in your language(s).

read sth. *v* German: ____________________

Your language(s): ____________________

1 Look at the pictures and write the school subjects.

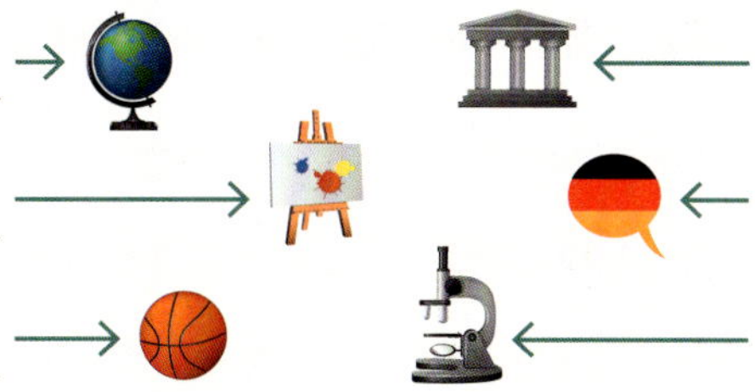

______________ ______________
______________ ______________
______________ ______________

2 What's the time? Tick the right answers.

1 12:15 ☐ quarter to twelve ☐ twelve past ten ☐ quarter past twelve
2 3:30 ☐ half past four ☐ half past three ☐ half past two
3 6:45 ☐ quarter past six ☐ half past seven ☐ quarter to seven
4 9.55 ☐ five to ten ☐ five past ten ☐ five to nine

3 Complete the text. Use the simple present.

Jo, Dev and Milly __________ **(go)** to Mercy School. School usually __________ **(start)** at 9 o'clock. The students at Mercy __________ **(wear)** school uniforms. They __________ **(not wear)** their own clothes. Milly __________ **(not like)** the school uniform. On Monday Jo __________ **(have)** two German lessons. Dev and Milly __________ **(not have)** German. They __________ **(learn)** French. In lessons 5 and 6 Mrs Fine __________ **(teach)** ICT. She always __________ **(go)** to the computer room with the class. School __________ **(finish)** at 3.30. After school Dev and Milly usually __________ **(do)** their homework. Jo __________ **(play)** football. He usually __________ **(do)** his homework after football training.

4 What can (✓) or can't (✗) they do? Read and write.

1 Taio and Ava ____________________
2 Taio ____________________
3 Ava ____________________
4 Taio and Ava ____________________

	T	A
speak German	✓	✓
spell 'geography'	✗	✓
take the maths test	✗	✗

English	German	My notes
Open your books at page 42.	Schlagt eure Bücher auf Seite 42 auf.	
Look at the timetable.	Schaue auf den Stundenplan./ Schaut ...	
Read page 32.	Lies Seite 32/Lest ...	
Can you read task 1, please?	Kannst du bitte Aufgabe 1 vorlesen?/Könnt ihr ...?	
Can you spell that word, please?	Kannst du bitte das Wort buchstabieren?/ Könnt ihr ...?	
Listen, please.	Hör bitte zu!/Hört bitte zu!	
(to) take a test	einen Test schreiben	
(to) do homework	Hausaufgaben machen	
(to) play football	Fuβball spielen	
(to) go to the gym	ins Fitness-Studio gehen	
(to) teach English (to) learn English (to) study English	Englisch unterrichten Englisch lernen Englisch üben, lernen	
(to) use a computer	einen Computer benutzen	
(to) speak English/German	Englisch/Deutsch sprechen	
I like PE (too). I don't like history.	Ich mag (auch) Sport. Ich mag Geschichte nicht.	

School subjects (Schulfächer)
art Kunst • **English** Englisch • **German** Deutsch • **geography** Geografie • **history** Geschichte • **ICT** Informatik • **maths** Mathe • **music** Musik • **PE** Sport • **science** Nawi

It's Tuesday.	Es ist Dienstag.	

The days of the week (Die Wochentage)
Monday Montag • **Tuesday** Dienstag • **Wednesday** Mittwoch • **Thursday** Donnerstag • **Friday** Freitag • **Saturday** Samstag • **Sunday** Sonntag

on Wednesdays on Wednesday	mittwochs, jeden Mittwoch am Mittwoch	
at the weekend	am Wochenende	

English	German	My notes
after school	nach der Schule	
What do we do every Tuesday?	Was machen wir jeden Dienstag?	
never	nie	
sometimes	manchmal	
usually	meistens, normalerweise	
every day	jeden Tag	
always	immer	
School starts at 8 o'clock. School finishes at 3:15.	Die Schule beginnt um 8 Uhr. Die Schule ist um 3:15 zu Ende.	

The numbers from 20 to 99 (Die Zahlen von 20 bis 99)
20 twenty, 21 twenty-one, 22 twenty-two, 23 twenty-three, …
29 twenty-nine
30 thirty 40 forty 50 fifty 60 sixty
70 seventy 80 eighty 90 ninety → Numbers, p. 111

from 9 **to** 11 o'clock	von 9 bis 11	

What's the time?	Wieviel Uhr ist es?
It's …	Es ist …
quarter past ten	Viertel nach zehn (*10:15 oder 22:15*)
half past ten	halb elf (*10:30 oder 22:30*)
quarter to eleven	Viertel vor elf (*10:45 oder 22:45*)

School things:	**Schulsachen:**	
pencil pen	der Bleistift der Kugelschreiber, der Stift, der Füller	
timetable	der Stundenplan	
exercise book	das Übungsheft	
computer	der Computer	
test	der Test	
lesson	die Unterrichtsstunde	
break	die Pause	
(to) wear a school uniform / your own clothes	eine Schuluniform / die eigene Kleidung tragen	
(to) get a mark	eine Note bekommen	

3 Family and friends

Family:
mother
father
brother
sister
cousin
best friend

→ My Words, pp. 40–41

◯ Yero, Olga's father and Yero's mother

◯ Olga, Mr Chan and Olga's cousin

◯ Mo, Mo's best friend and a classmate

1 A class party with family and friends

a 🔊32–34 📖 Listen to and read the dialogues 1–3.

b 📖 ✏ Find the groups of people on page 30 and number them (1–3).

1

Mr Chan: Good morning, I'm Olga's teacher. And who are you? Are you Olga's mother?

Dina: No, I'm Olga's cousin Dina. Olga's father, Mr Orlow, is the man over there.

Olga: Look, Mr Chan. This is my mother. And this is my big sister. They live in Russia.

2

Nico: Where do you sit, Mo?

Mo: I usually sit here.

Nico: Cool. What do you usually do in your English lessons?

Mo: We talk, we watch videos …

Classmate: And we make videos.

Nico: Videos? That's so cool! I'm so bored at my school. Why can't we make videos?

3

Yero: Do you like our chillout zone, Mr Orlow? The blue sofa is old and the white shelves are new.

Mr Orlow: Yes, I do.

Yero: And you, Mum? What do you like most about our chillout zone?

Mrs Touré: I like the colours most. And I like your birthday calendar.

c 📖 Match the questions to the answers. Check your answers in dialogues 1–3.

1 Where does Olga's mum live?
2 Who is Nico?
3 Why is Nico bored at his school?
4 Does Mr Orlow like the chillout zone?
5 What does Mrs Touré like most about the chillout zone?

A He is Mo's best friend.
B Yes, he does.
C She likes the colours most.
D She lives in Russia.
E Because they don't make videos at his school.

party
Who are you?
man
big sister
(to) live (in)

Where do you sit?
Why can't we make videos?
(to) be bored
(to) talk (to sb./about sth.)
(to) make
(to) watch
cool
Do you like our chillout zone?
Yes, I do.
No, I don't.
birthday calendar
sofa
shelf, *pl* shelves
new
What do you like most about …?
because

English and German

when?	wann?
what?	was?
where?	wo?
why?	warum?
who?	wer?

→ My Words, pp. 40–41

1 The simple present: questions and short answers

a 35 Listen and read.

Olga: Do you like the new furniture, Mr Chan?
Mr Chan: Yes, I do. And do you like it, Olga?
Olga: Yes, I do. What about Jill? Does she like it?
Mr Chan: Yes, she does. And Mo and Yero?
Do they like the new furniture?
Olga: Yero does, but Mo doesn't.
He doesn't like the colours.
Mr Chan: That's too bad!

b Read the boxes. Then mark in the dialogue in 1a: questions with *do* and short answers.

Do	I you we you they	like the furniture? make videos?
Does	he/she/it Mo	like the colours?

Yes,	I/you we/you/they	do.
No,		don't.
Yes,	he/she/it	does.
No,		doesn't.

c Write five questions about your school in your exercise book.

Do you like	the birthday calendar • break time • the shelves • the sofa • the tables • the chillout zone • …	in our classroom? at our school?

d Ask a partner. Write down his or her answers in your exercise book.

Questions	*My partner's answers*
Do you like the shelves in our classroom?	*Yes, I do.*

2 The simple present: questions and short answers with *be* and *can*

Read the box. Write questions and answer them in your exercise book.

⚠ Never use *do* with *be* or *can*:
Are you Olga's mother? — No, I'm not.
Can you see Olga's father? — Yes, I can.

→ Module 1, pp. 6–7 (be); Module 2, p. 19 (can)

1 nice | your classmates | Are | ?
2 your classroom | new | Is | ?
3 watch | Can | videos | in class | you | ?
4 Can | your smartphones | use | you | in class | ?

1. Are your classmates nice? – Yes, they are.

3 The simple present: questions with question words

a 36 Listen and read.

b Find the question words in 3a and mark them in different colours:
what, when, why, who

c Read the boxes. Write the questions from 3a in the table.

Questions with question words:
What do I like best?
Where do you go?
When does school start?
Why does he like the chillout zone?

Question words with *be* and *can*:
Who are you?
When is your birthday?
What can you see?
When are you bored?

Questions with question words + *do*	Questions with question words only
What do you	*When are you*

d Choose three questions from 3a (you can change the green words).
Ask a classmate or a friend. Write the questions and answers in your exercise book.

Questions	*My partner's answers*
What do you do on Sundays?	*I usually play basketball on Saturdays.*

Family:
mother – mum
father – dad
brother
sister
grandmother – grandma
grandfather – grandpa
aunt
uncle
cousin
good friend

my
your
his
her
our
their

1 Family and good friends

a 🔊37 ✎ Look at Olga's family photos. Listen and write the family words.

1	mother	5	______	9	______
2	______	6	______	10	______
3	______	7	______	11	______
4	______	8	______		

English and German
Jill's family photo
Jills Familienfoto

partner
half-brother / half-sister
great
happy
little brother ↔
big brother

b 🔊38 ✎ Look at Jill's family photo. Listen and number.

c 🔊39 ✎ Listen and complete the text.

aunt's • cool • dad's • little • great • happy • has •
He's • ~~mum's~~ • new partner • She's

Short and long forms
He's five. = He **is** five.
She's cool. = She **is** cool.

My mum's name is Mary. She has a ________, Henry. My ________ half-brother's name is Oliver. ______ five. He always looks ______.
My ______ name is Jane. ______ really ______. She ______ red hair.
My ______ name is Pete. He's ______! He sends me funny messages every day.

d ✎ Write in your exercise book about a friend or a family member.

My sister's name is ... She's ...

→ My Words, pp. 40–41

2 The birthday calendar

a 🔊40 📖 Listen to and read the months in the margin.
b 🔊41 ✏ Listen to the dialogue. Write about Mo, Olga and Yero's birthdays.

HAPPY BIRTHDAY!

5th January	*Mo*
8th February	*Selina*
12th April	*Jill*
20th June	*Mr Chan*
31st July	*Yero*
3rd August	*Olga*
11th August	*Nino*

Jill: *It's in April. It's on the twelfth of April.*

Mo: ____________________

Olga: ____________________

Yero: ____________________

c ✏ Write about your birthday in your exercise book. Check online about celebrities with the same birthday.

My birthday is in ... It's on the ... .
These celebrities have the same birthday: ...

When's your birthday?
It's in June.
It's on the twelfth of June.

Months:
January
February
March
April
May
June
July
August
September
October
November
December

Ordinal numbers:
1st first
2nd second
3rd third
4th fourth
5th fifth
6th sixth
7th seventh
8th eighth
9th ninth
10th tenth
11th eleventh
12th twelfth
13th thirteenth
14th fourteenth
15th fifteenth
16th sixteenth
17th seventeenth
18th eighteenth
19th nineteenth
20th twentieth
21st twenty-first
...

3 A birthday invitation

a 📖 Read. Then match the questions to the answers.

INVITATION – It's my birthday.

Date: Saturday, 5th July
Place: at the youth club

Time: from 4.00 to 8.30 pm
See you at my party!
Yero

1 What's this?
2 Why does Yero celebrate?
3 Where does he celebrate?
4 When is the party?

A Because it's his birthday.
B It's on Saturday, the fifth of July.
C It's a birthday invitation.
D He celebrates at the youth club.

(to) celebrate

4 Thinking about languages

a ✏ 💬 Write the months in your language(s) and say them.
b 👥 💬 Compare with your classmates.

→ Numbers, p. 111
→ My Words, pp. 40–41

Furniture:
chair
shelf, *pl* shelves
sofa
table
rug
cushion

5 Furniture

a 42 Listen and look. Write down the furniture words 1–6.

1 ____________ 4 ____________
2 ____________ 5 ____________
3 ____________ 6 ____________

a chair • a shelf • a sofa • a table • a rug • a cushion

Singular and plural
There**'s** (**is**) a rug.
There **are** five chairs.

b Look at the picture in 3a again. Complete the text with the singular or plural of the furniture words.

I really like the chillout zone in our classroom. There's a big yellow ______ in the middle. There are also ________ in different colours. There's an old blue ______ on the left. There are big green __________ on the sofa. Here we can sit and read or relax. There are white ________ for our books. And there are small, old ________ on the left and right.

on the left
on the right
in the middle

small

c 43 Listen and check.

d Draw your dream chillout zone and write about it. You can use the ideas from the box.

→ Module 1, p. 15 (colours)

There are	cool • big • blue • green • new • nice • old • red • small • yellow • …	chairs • cushions • rugs • sofas • shelves • tables • …	on the left. on the right. in the middle.
There is a		chair • cushion • rug • sofa • table • …	

This is my dream chillout zone.
There are cool big cushions on the left …

→ My Words, pp. 40–41

6 An interview

a Find out interesting things about people in your class or at your school. Make a table and write down questions.

	Me	Partner 1	Partner 2
1 Who is your favourite celebrity?			
2 What is your favourite music?			
3 When are you bored?			
4 Where are you from?			
5 Do you like school?			
6 Do you have brothers or sisters?			
7 ...			

teacher • ...

month • school subject • ...

happy• ...

are your parents • is your best friend • ...

English • maths • pizza • ...

cousins • aunts • uncles • ...

TIP: Change the green words in the questions:
Who is your favourite celebrity?
→ *Who is your favourite teacher?*

(to) be interested in sth.

TIP: You can look up more words in an online dictionary or in the online English-German dictionary for this workbook.

b Ask people in a friendly way.

c Write your partners' answers in your table.

Questions	*Me*	*Partner 1: Nahla*
1. Who is your favourite celebrity?	*Lucas Torreira*	*Jimin from BTS*
2. What is your favourite music?	*pop*	

Reporting
Nahla: "My favourite celebrity is Jimin."
→ *Nahla's/Her favourite celebrity is Jimin.*

Theo: "My favourite music is rap."
→ *Theo's/His favourite music is rap.*

d Write down people's answers in full sentences. Report to the class.

1. My favourite celebrity is Lucas Torreira. Nahla's favourite celebrity is Jimin from BTS.
2. My favourite music is pop. Her favourite music is ...

→ My Words, pp. 40–41

TIP: You don't need to understand every word.

1 Understanding new words

a Look at the brochures.

GREEN LIFE

Great ideas for birthday presents. Make teens happy with these birthday presents.

All our ideas are friendly to the environment!

MODERN SCHOOL

Bored with grey chairs and tables in your classroom? Check out our high-top tables and stools! Try our colourful pouffes.

Work at our high-top tables. You can stand or sit on stools. And during break time relax on pouffes.

TIP: How to understand new words:
1. Look at the pictures.
2. Do you understand a part of the word?
3. Think about other languages.
4. Check the context of the word.

b Try to understand the marked words in the brochures. Use these tips:

1. Look at the pictures.

water bottles

2. You know one part of the word. Can you guess the other part?

friendly: friend + ly

3. Think about words in other languages.

chocolate:
Schokolade, czekolada, cioccolata, çikolata, chocolat, ...

4. Check the context of the word. Can you guess the other part?

Work at our high-top tables.
You can **stand or sit** on stools.

c Write the marked words from 1a in English, German and your language(s) in your exercise book.

English	*German*	*Your language(s)*
water bottle	*(die) Wasserflasche*	
...		

d Check the words in a dictionary.

1 Write the questions and answer them.

1 you | school | ~~Do~~ | like | ?

Do ____________________ ____________________

2 two languages | speak | your family | Does | ?

____________________ ____________________

3 your friends | Do | videos | watch | ?

____________________ ____________________

2 Complete the questions with *why*, *what*, *when* and *where*.

1 ________ is this? This is an invitation.

2 ________ is the party? The party is at school.

3 ________ is the party? It's next Friday.

4 ________ do we celebrate? Because we have a new classroom.

3 44 Listen and write down the family words.

1 ____________ 6 ____________

2 ____________ 7 ____________

3 ____________ 8 ____________

4 ____________ 9 ____________

5 ____________

4 Complete the sentences.

When is your birthday? My birthday is in ____________________.

My birthday is on ____________________.

5 Write down five or more furniture words.

____

____

English	German	My notes
Family and friends:	**Familie und Freunde:**	
mother – mum father – dad	die Mutter – Mama der Vater – Papa	
brother sister	der Bruder die Schwester	
half-brother half-sister	der Halbbruder die Halbschwester	
grandmother – grandma grandfather – grandpa	die Großmutter – Oma der Großvater – Opa	
aunt uncle	die Tante der Onkel	
cousin	der Cousin/die Cousine	
partner	der Partner/die Partnerin	
best friend	der beste Freund/ die beste Freundin	
man, *pl* men woman, *pl* women	der Mann, *Pl.* die Männer die Frau, *Pl.* die Frauen	
my, your, his, her, our, their **my mother** meine Mutter • **your father** dein/euer Vater • **his uncle** sein Onkel • **her brother** ihr Bruder • **our aunt** unsere Tante • **their cousin** ihre Cousine		
because	weil	
party	die Party	
Describing people/things (Personen/Dinge beschreiben) **bored** gelangweilt • **cool** cool, toll • **good** gut • **great** großartig, toll • **nice** nett, hübsch • **big** *(age, size)* groß • **little** *(age, size)* klein • **small** *(size)* klein • **happy** glücklich, froh • **new** neu • **old** alt		
(to) live (in)	leben, wohnen (in)	
(to) talk (to sb./about sth.)	reden (mit jm./über etwas)	
(to) watch (a video)	(ein Video) anschauen	
(to) make	machen	
(to) celebrate	feiern	
on the left/on the right in the middle	links / rechts in der Mitte	

English	German	My notes
Who are you?	Wer bist du?/Wer sind Sie?	
Who is your favourite celebrity?	Wer ist deine liebste Prominente/dein liebster Prominenter?	
What do you like most about …?	Was magst du am meisten an …?/Was mögen Sie …?	
Where do you sit?	Wo sitzt du?/Wo sitzen Sie?	
When are you bored?	Wann ist dir/Ihnen langweilig?	
Why can't we make videos?	Warum können wir keine Videos machen?	
Do you like …? Yes, I do./No, I don't.	Magst du …?/Mögen Sie …? Ja./Nein.	

Months (Monate)
January Januar • **February** Februar • **March** März • **April** April • **May** Mai• **June** Juni • **July** Juli • **August** August • **September** September • **October** Oktober • **November** November • **December** Dezember

When's your birthday? My birthday is **in May**. My birthday is **on the twelfth of June**.	Wann hast du Geburtstag? Ich habe im Mai Geburtstag. Ich habe am zwölften Juni Geburtstag.	
birthday calendar	der Geburtstagskalender	

Ordinal numbers (Ordinalzahlen)
1st first der/die/das erste, **2nd second**, **3rd third**, **4th fourth**, **5th fifth**, **6th sixth**, **7th seventh**, **8th eighth**, **9th ninth**, **10th tenth**, **11th eleventh**, **12th twelfth**, **20th twentieth**, **21st twenty-first**, …

→ Numbers, p. 111

Furniture:	**Möbel:**	
chair	der Stuhl	
table	der Tisch	
shelf, *pl* shelves	das Regal, *Pl.* die Regale	
rug	der Teppich	
sofa	das Sofa	
cushion	das Kissen	

Where were you
last weekend?

I was at the youth club.

I was at home.

What did you do?

I played football.

I watched football on TV.

It was fun/great/
very exciting.

Was it fun?

Yes, it was.

No, it wasn't.

at the youth club

(to) practise

(to) dance

(to) stop

(to) cheer

(to) play football

(to) win a match,
simple past: won

(to) watch (TV, a film)

(to) have a cold,
simple past: had

(to) do sport,
simple past: did

(to) be at home,
simple past: was, were

(to) go to bed early,
simple past: went

but
then
because
lots of

→ My Words, pp. 54–55

1 What did they do last weekend?

a 45 Look at page 42. Listen to and read the dialogue.

b Who did what? Match the sentences to the pictures.

1 She practised with her drama group.

2 He watched football on TV.

3 He danced with his friends.

4 He played football.

Picture A

Picture B

Picture C

Picture D

c How was it? Read again. Tick the right answers.

	Yes, it was.	No, it wasn't.
1 Olga's weekend was exciting.	☐	☑
2 Mo's weekend was great.	☐	☐
3 Mr Chan's weekend was fun.	☐	☐
4 Yero's weekend was OK.	☐	☐

2 More free-time activities

a 46 Look at the pictures and listen. Listen again and repeat.

1 
play video games

2 
take photos

3 
listen to music

4 
visit your grandma

5 
meet friends

6 
chat with friends

b What did they do yesterday? Complete the sentences.

chatted • listened • met • ~~played~~ • took • visited

1 Basar and Jo *played* video games.

2 Mia ____ photos in the park.

3 Cero ____ to music.

4 Sandra ____ her grandma.

5 Milan ____ his friends in a cafe.

6 Sue ____ with her best friend.

c 47 Listen and check.

Free-time activities:
(to) visit your grandma
(to) play video games
(to) take photos (of)
(to) listen to music
(to) meet friends
(to) chat with friends

yesterday
in the park

→ My Words, pp. 54–55

1 The simple past: positive statements

a Read about the simple past with regular verbs.
Then complete the sentences with the simple past of the verbs.

I You He/She/It We You They	practised. danced. played.

You form the simple past of regular verbs with -ed.

⚠ Be careful with the spelling of these verbs:
practise, dance: practised, danced
chat, stop: chatted, stopped
study: studied (but: play – played)

I studied for the English test yesterday.
Last weekend we visited my grandmother.
I played football with my friends on Sunday.

You use the simple past to say what you did or what happened in the past.
Signal words: yesterday, last week, last year, on Monday, at 8 o'clock, …

1 I ____________ **(play)** video games yesterday.
2 Mo ____________ **(chat)** with Yero last Friday.
3 They ____________ **(watch)** TV yesterday.
4 Olga ____________ **(study)** last weekend.
5 School ____________ **(start)** at 8 o'clock.
6 I ____________ **(dance)** on Saturday.

b Mark the signal words in sentences 1–6.

c Read about the simple past with irregular verbs. Write the simple past forms in the table.
(You can find them on pages 42–43.)

I You He/She/It We You They	had a cold. was at home. met friends.

There is no rule for the simple past of irregular verbs. You need to learn them.

→ Irregular verbs, pp. 108–109

irregular verb	simple past
be	was, were
have	____________
meet	____________
take	____________
win	____________

d Complete the text with the simple past of the regular verbs and irregular verbs.

Jill ________ **(have)** a nice weekend. On Saturday morning she ________ **(chat)** online with her dad. They ________ **(talk)** about their favourite rugby teams. Then she ________ **(watched)** a rugby game at the stadium. A team from her club ________ **(play)** – and they ________ **(win)**. She ________ **(take)** lots of photos. She ________ **(show)** her photos to the players and they ________ **(like)** them. Jill ________ **(be)** very happy!

3 The simple past: negative statements

a Read the box. Then complete the sentences with the negative forms of the verbs in the box.

I You He/She/It We You They	didn't (= did not)	practise. dance. go.

You make negative statements in the simple past with didn't and the infinitive of the verb:
He didn't watch TV.

⚠ **not:** He didn't ~~watched~~ TV

chat • do • met • play • watch

1 Yero ______________ TV yesterday.

2 Mr Chan ______________ sport at the weekend.

3 Olga ______________ with her cousin on Saturday.

4 Mo ______________ video games on Sunday.

b At the weekend Yero had a list of things to do. Read Yero's list. Write what he didn't do.

1 *Yero didn't do his maths homework.*

2 *He* ______________

3 ______________

4 ______________

5 ______________

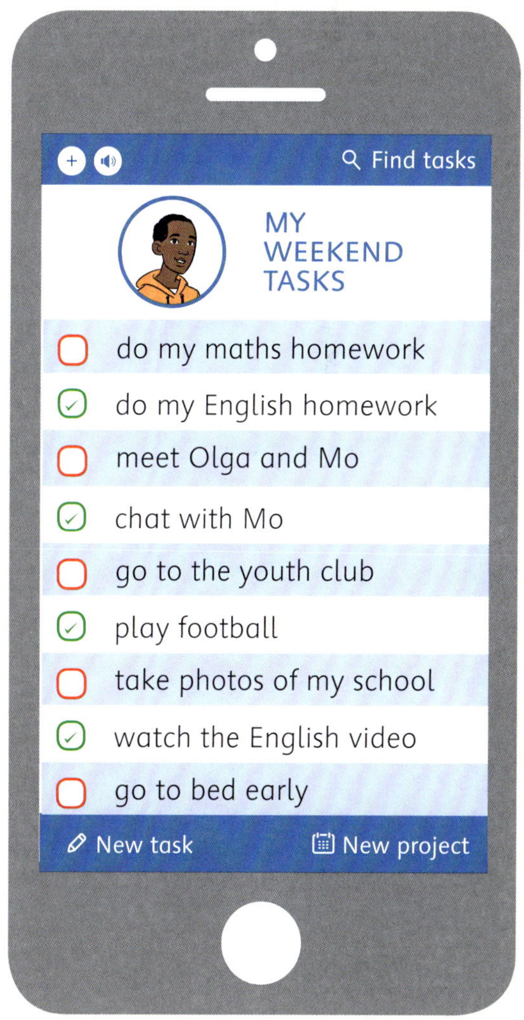

c Read again. Write what Yero did. Use positive sentences.(Look at page 44 for help.)

1 *Yero did his* ______________

2 *He* ______________

3 ______________

4 ______________

d What did you do last weekend? Write three sentences in your exercise book.

I visited my aunt, ...

e Compare your sentences with a partner.

3 The simple past: questions and short answers

a Read the boxes. Write four or more questions in your exercise book and answer them.

Did	I you he/she/it we you they	watch a film? stop? meet friends?

Yes,	I/you he/she/it we/you/they	did.
No,	I/you he/she/it we/you/they	didn't.

Did	you you and your friends	go to the youth club • play football / video games • do sport • meet friends • listen to music • watch a film • …	last weekend? yesterday?

Did you go to the youth club last weekend? – No, I didn't.

b Ask and answer the questions with a partner.

4 The simple past: questions with question words

a Read the boxes. Then write the questions and answer them.

What Where When	did	I you he/she/it we you they	watch? meet? stop?

Questions	**Answers**
How did you like it? What did you watch?	I liked it very much. We watched a film.
The verb forms *like*, *watch* are infinitives.	The verb forms *liked*, *watched* are simple past forms.

1 ~~Where~~ | yesterday | you | ~~did~~ | go | ?

Where did ______ *I went* ______

2 you | did | What | do | ?

______ *I/We* ______

3 like best | What | did | you | ?

______ ______

4 to bed | When | go | you | did | ?

______ *I* ______

5 The simple past of the verb *be*: positive and negative statements

a Read the boxes. Then mark the right words in the sentences:
was, *were*, *wasn't* or *weren't*.

I He/She/It Yero/Jill	was	at home.
You We They	were	at home.

I He/She/It Yero/Jill	wasn't	at home.
You We They	weren't	at home.

1 Mo's dance contest **was/were** at the park.

2 Mr Chan **wasn't/weren't** at the theatre.

3 Yero's friends **was/were** at the stadium.

4 The students **wasn't/weren't** at school

5 Olga **was/were** at the youth club.

6 Mr Chan and his friend **was/were** at home.

6 The simple past of the verb *be*: questions and short answers

a Read the boxes. Then match the questions to the answers.

Was	I He/She/It Yero/Jill	at home?
Were	You We They	at home?

Yes,	I/you he/she/it	was.
No,		wasn't.
Yes,	we/you/they	were.
No,		weren't.

Questions with question words:
How was your weekend?
Who was there?
When were you at home?

1 How was your weekend?

2 Where were you?

3 Who was with you?

4 Why did you go there?

5 Was the film good?

6 When were you home again?

7 Was Dina with you?

A My cousin Dina.

B Because they showed a film about Russia.

C It was very nice.

D No, she wasn't.

E I was at the youth club.

F I was at home at 10 o'clock.

G Yes, it was!

b 48 Listen to the dialogue and check your answers.

TIP: How to understand new words:
1. Look at the pictures.
2. Think about other languages.
3. Do you understand parts of the word?
4. Check the context of the word.

→ Module 3, p. 38 (Understanding new words)

(very) popular
(to) do exercises
training
first
(to) love sth./sb.

1 Jill's weekend blog

a 49 Listen to and read Jill's blog.

JILL'S WEEKEND BLOG

Home

Last weekend I was at a rugby camp. In Britain rugby is a very popular team sport. In Germany rugby isn't very popular. But I was lucky: there's a rugby club in my German hometown!
In a rugby game there are two teams of 15 players. They play with an oval ball and two H-shaped goals. The team that scores more points wins the game. Read more about rugby

5th May
Training started at 5 pm. First we did special exercises.
Read more about our exercises

6th May
We learned lots of new rugby skills. It was very hard. But we had lots of fun too!
Read more about rugby skills

7th May
The girls were so great! I just love my team!
Read more about my rugby team

rugby, fun, sports, camp, training

like comment share 0 comments

b Read again. Match the dates to the titles.

1 5th May
2 6th May
3 7th May

A What we learned
B My team was great!
C A good start

c Read again. Tick the right answers.

1 Jill was at a …	◯ rugby camp.	◯ rugby match.
2 Rugby is very popular in …	◯ Germany.	◯ Britain.
3 Training started on …	◯ 5th May.	◯ 5th March.
4 The girls learned lots of …	◯ new subjects.	◯ new skills.

→ My Words, pp. 54–55

2 Sports week at school

a 50 Who did what sport? Listen and read. Write letters: *M* for Mo, *O* for Olga and *Y* for Yero.

O
do exercises

play chess

play table tennis

do kung fu

go skateboarding

go swimming

b Write positive sentences. Use the simple past of *do*, *play* and *go*.

1 *Olga did exercises and*

2 *Mo*

3 *Yero*

c What didn't they do? Write negative sentences.

1 *Olga didn't play chess, go swimming, do kung fu or play table tennis.*

2 *Mo*

3 *Yero*

Sports:
(to) play table tennis
(to) do exercises
(to) go skateboarding
(to) do kung fu
(to) play chess
(to) go swimming

Positive and negative statements
Mo **played** chess.
Mo **didn't play** chess.

English and German
I **listened** to music.
Ich **habe** Musik **gehört**.
Ich **hörte** Musik.

You **listened** to music.
Du **hast** Musik **gehört**.
Du **hörtest** Musik.

She **listened** to music.
Sie **hat** Musik **gehört**.
Sie **hörte** Musik.

3 Thinking about cultures

a What sports are popular in your home country or in other countries? Talk to a partner.

b Choose one sport and find more information about it:
- How many players are there?
- Who wins the game?
- ...

c Tell your partner about your sport.

→ My Words, pp. 54–55

4 Last week was different

a Read. Mark the right verb forms: simple present or simple past.

Last week Mr Chan **have/had** a cold. He **isn't/wasn't** at school and so lots of things **are/were** different. We usually **have/had** English on Tuesdays and Thursdays. But last week we **don't have/didn't have** English on Tuesday. We **have/had** maths with Mrs Kern. Olga **is/was** happy because she **likes/liked** maths. We often **watch/watched** English videos with Mr Chan. But Mrs Kern **doesn't watch/didn't watch** a video with us. She **does/did** a maths test! On Thursday we **have/had** English with Jill. It **is/was** really cool! We **listen/listened** to music and we **make/made** our own songs. Jill **records/recorded** our songs so Mr Chan can listen to them.

different
so
(to) make,
simple past: made

b 51 Listen and check.

5 Mr Chan had a cold last week

Simple present and simple past

Use the **simple present** to say what usually, always, never happens:
I **go**, you **play**, he/she/it **likes**, …

→ Module 2, pp. 18–19

Use the **simple past** to say what happened yesterday, last week, …:
I **went**, you **played**, he/she/it **liked**, …

a What didn't Mr Chan do last week? Look and write.

1  ✗

2  ✗

3  ✗

4  ✗

1 *He didn't go* ______ (not go swimming)

2 ______ (not play video games)

3 ______ (not go to school)

4 ______ (not do exercises)

b What didn't you do last week? Write three sentences or more in your exercise book.

I didn't	play do go	football • table tennis • video games • … exercises • my homework • sport • … swimming • to bed early • to school • …	last week.

I didn't do exercises last week.

→ My Words, pp. 54–55

c Compare your sentences with a partner.

6 Your blog post *A great day*

a Collect your ideas in this mind map. You can use ideas from the boxes.

A great day

1 When?
last weekend • last Saturday • yesterday • …

____

____

2 Who?
my friends • my cousin • …

____

____

3 Where?
at home • in the park • at the youth club • …

____

____

4 What?
danced • met friends • played chess • watched films • …

____

____

5 How?
(very) exciting • great • fun • …

____

____

TIP: Look up words in an online dictionary or in the English-German dictionary for this workbook.

b Write your blog post. Use your ideas from 6a.

posted by ______________ on ______________________

1 ______________________ I had a great day!

2 I was with ______________________

3 We were ______________________

4 We ______________________

____

5 It was ______________________

like comment share

c Interview your partner about his or her great day. Ask these questions:

1 When was your great day?
2 Who was with you?
3 Where were you?
4 What did you do?
5 How was it?
6 …

Reporting
Sirin: "Last weekend I had a great day."
→ *Last weekend Sirin had a great day.*

d Write about your partner's day in your exercise book.

Last Sunday Ira had a great day. She was with …

→ My Words, pp. 54–55

Dear
Hello
Hi
Love
Best wishes

(to) have to,
simple past: had to

1 How to write better emails

a Read Jill's emails. How can you start and finish an email? Write the words from the box on the right line.

Start an email: ______________________

Finish an email: ______________________

Best wishes • Dear • Hello • Hi • Love

Subject: An exciting week!
Hi Dad
How are you? How was your week? Last week Mr Chan had a cold, so I had to teach English and Mrs Kern taught the other subjects. It was very exciting because on Thursday I was alone with the class! First we listened to music and talked about it. Then the kids made their own songs. They were really good and I think they liked my English lesson!
What did you do? Please write soon!
Love
Jill

Subject: Last week!
Dear Mr Chan
How are you?
Last week was special because we had to manage without you. First the students weren't happy because they like your English lessons best. But then they were OK. On Thursday we listened to some music and then students made their own songs.
The students say hello to you.
Get well soon.
Best wishes
Jill Corothers

b Find these words in the emails in 1a and mark them with the right colour:

Time words:
last weekend, on Thursday, first, then

Linking words:
and, but, because, so

TIP: Use time words and linking words to make your text interesting.
time words: last weekend, on Monday/..., first, then, ...
linking words: and, but, so, because, ...

TIP: You can use ideas from p. 51.

c Write an email to a friend or a teacher about last weekend. (Write on the computer or in your exercise book.)

1 Write the subject on the subject line.
2 Start the email with *Dear* or *Hello*.
3 Ask questions.
4 Write about what you did last weekend. Use the simple past.
5 Use time words and linking words.
6 Finish the email with *Best wishes* or *Love* and your name.

Subject: ... 1
Dear/Hello ... 2
How are you? 3
Last weekend I went ... 4
First ... and then ... because ... 5
How was your weekend? 3
Love/Best wishes ... 6

d Check your text with your teacher or a partner.

→ My Words, pp. 54–55

1 Write the sports and activities under the pictures.

go ______ ______ ______ ______

2 Complete the dialogue with *was*, *were*, *wasn't*, *weren't*.

Taio: Hi, Ava! How ______ **(1)** your weekend?

Ava: It ______ **(2)** OK, thanks. My best friend and I ______ **(3)** at a concert.

Taio: ______ **(4)** it fun?

Ava: No, it ______ **(5)**. I ______ **(6)** there very early, but my friend ______ **(7)**. Then my friend ______ **(8)** there, but the band ______ **(9)**! The concert started two hours late.

Taio: ______ **(10)** the music good?

Ava: It ______ **(11)** OK. It ______ **(12)** my favourite style of music.

3 Complete the text with the regular and irregular simple past forms.

Yesterday Yero and Mo ______ **(go)** to the stadium because their favourite football team ______ **(play)**. The match ______ **(be)** very exciting. Their team ______ **(win)** 2:0. Yero and Mo ______ **(cheer)** and ______ **(take)** lots of photos. Later they ______ **(watch)** the best scenes on their smartphones and ______ **(talk)** about football for hours.

4 Mark the right words.

Dear/Hi Mrs Kern
Thank you for your help with my English lesson **next/last** week. Your tips were very useful for me. **Then/First** I played English raps **but/because** the students like music. **Yesterday/Then** the students worked in groups **and/but** made songs.

Love/Best wishes
Jillian Corothers

English	German	My notes
What did you do last weekend?	Was hast du letztes Wochenende gemacht?/ Was haben Sie …?	
How was your weekend?	Wie war dein/Ihr Wochenende?	
Where were you?	Wo warst du?/ Wo waren Sie?	
Was it fun? Yes, it was. / No, it wasn't.	Hat es Spaß gemacht? Ja. / Nein.	

It was … / It's … (Es war … / Es ist …)
different anders(artig) • **exciting** aufregend, spannend • **great** großartig, toll • **OK** OK • **(very) popular** (sehr) beliebt • **It was fun.** Es hat Spaß gemacht.

training	das Training	
lots of sport/things/…	viel Sport/viele Dinge/…	
(to) practise	üben	
(to) love sth./sb.	etwas/jn. lieben	
(to) stop	aufhören	
(to) cheer	jubeln	
(to) watch a film	einen Film schauen	
(to) win a match	ein Match/ein Spiel gewinnen	
(to) have a cold	eine Erkältung haben	
(to) have to do sth.	etwas tun müssen	
(to) go to bed early	früh ins Bett gehen	

Irregular simple past forms

be	**was/were**	sein: war, ist gewesen
do	**did**	tun: tat, hat getan
go	**went**	gehen: ging, ist gegangen
have	**had**	haben: hatte, hat gehabt
make	**made**	machen: machte, hat gemacht
meet	**met**	treffen: traf, hat getroffen
take	**took**	nehmen: nahm, hat genommen
win	**won**	gewinnen: gewann, hat gewonnen

→ Irregular verbs, pp. 108–109

English	German	My notes
at the youth club	im Jugendzentrum	
at home	zu Hause	
in the park	im Park	

Linking words (Konjunktionen, Verbindungswörter)
and und • **because** weil • **but** aber • **so** also, daher
Time words (Zeitadverbien)
first zuerst • **then** dann • **yesterday** gestern • **last week** letzte Woche • **last weekend** letztes Wochenende

Sports and other free-time activities:	**Sport und andere Freizeitaktivitäten:**	
(to) dance	tanzen	
(to) play football	Fußball spielen	
(to) play table tennis	Tischtennis spielen	
(to) play chess	Schach spielen	
(to) play video games	Videospiele spielen	
(to) do sport	Sport machen	
(to) go swimming	schwimmen gehen	
(to) go skateboarding	Skateboard fahren	
(to) do kung fu	Kung Fu machen	
(to) do exercises	Übungen/Gymnastik machen	
(to) visit your grandma	die Oma besuchen	
(to) take photos (of)	Fotos machen (von)	
(to) listen to music	Musik hören	
(to) meet friends	Freunde treffen	
(to) chat with friends	mit Freunden chatten (*per Internet*); reden, plaudern	

Writing emails and letters (E-Mails und Briefe schreiben)
Dear … Liebe(r) … • **Hi** … Hi … • **Hello** … Hallo … • **Best wishes** Viele Grüße • **Love** Alles Liebe

5 Getting around town

What are you doing?

I'm lying under my favourite tree in the park.

Are you having fun?

No, I'm not. / Yes, I am.

at the moment

(right) now

today

Getting around town:

(to) sit at the bus stop

(to) wait for the bus

(to) go to the park / the cinema

(to) look for a bus ticket (in a rucksack)

(to) help sb.

(to) come

(to) stand in the queue

(to) buy snacks

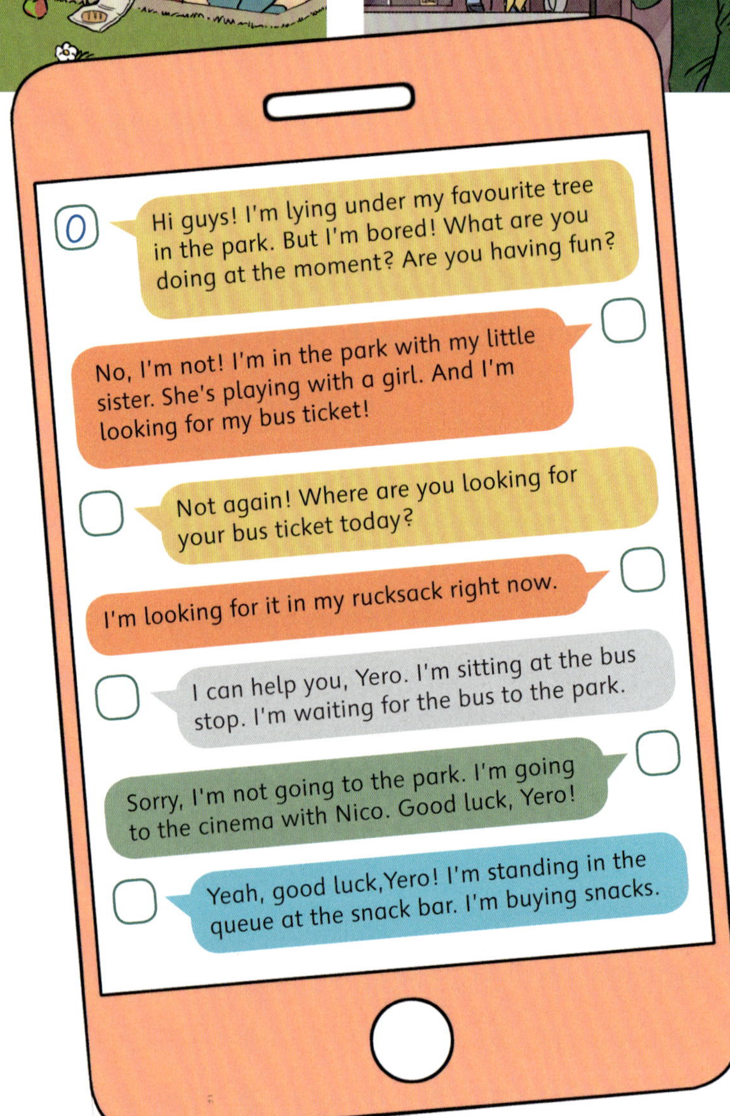

→ My Words, pp. 66–67

1 I'm looking for my bus ticket!

a 52 Look at page 56. Listen and read.

b Read page 56 again and look at the pictures. Write *O* for Olga, *M* for Mo, *Y* for Yero, *D* for Dina and *N* for Nico.

c What are they doing? Match the pictures to the sentences.

I'm going to the cinema with Nico.	I'm looking for my bus ticket.	I'm waiting for the bus to the park.	I'm lying under my favourite tree in the park.

2 What are they doing?

a 53 Look and listen. Number the sentences (1–6).

1 

2 

3 

4 

5 

6 

(to) get ready for school
(to) drink water
(to) eat a sandwich
(to) read a book
(to) talk to each other

- ◯ Leo is drinking water.
- ◯ Sam is reading a book.
- (1) Max is chatting with a friend.
- ◯ Gabrielle is eating a sandwich.
- ◯ Lily is getting ready for school.
- ◯ Pina and Greta are talking to each other.

b What are your classmates doing now?
Write four or more sentences in your exercise book.

Lisa and Jakob are getting ready for maths.
Hasan is eating a sandwich.

TIP: Change the green words in the sentences from 2a:
Gabrielle is eating a sandwich.
→ *Leo and Greta are eating a pizza.*

→ My Words, pp. 66–67

1 The present progressive: positive statements

a Read the boxes. Then complete the sentences with the present progressive of the verbs.

I'm (= am) You're (= are) He/She/It's (= is) We're You're They're	waiting. listening. reading.	You form the present progressive with am, are, is and the -ing form of the verb. ⚠ Be careful with the spelling of these verbs: come, write: coming, writing chat, get, sit: chatting, getting, sitting lie: lying

I'm listening to music at the moment. I'm talking to my best friend now. The people (in the picture) are talking to each other.	You use the present progressive to say what somebody is doing now. You also use it to say what people are doing in pictures. signal words: now, at the moment, …

1 Yero *is* ____________ **(look for)** his bus ticket.

2 Olga ____________ **(help)** Yero.

3 The little girls ____________ **(sit)** in the playground.

4 They ____________ **(play)** at the moment.

5 Now Dina ____________ **(come)** to the playground.

b Find the signal words in sentences 1–5 and mark them.

2 The present progressive: negative statements

a Read the box. Then complete the sentences with the present progressive of the verbs.

I'm not … You aren't … He/She/It isn't We aren't You aren't They aren't	waiting. listening. reading.

1 Yero's sister ____________ **(not look for)** the bus ticket.

2 Mo and Nico ____________ **(not go)** to the park.

3 Yero and Olga ____________ **(not talk)**.

4 Yero ____________ **(not have)** fun today.

b Look at the picture in 1. Where is Yero's bus ticket? Write and tick.

The bus ticket ____________ **(lie)** under … ◯ the rucksack. ◯ the books. ◯ the apple.

3 The present progressive: questions and short answers

a 54 Listen and read.

Dina: Hi, Yero. Are you still looking for your ticket?
Yero: Yes, I am.
Dina: Is your sister helping you?
Yero: No, she isn't. She's playing. But Olga is helping.
Dina: Where is she looking for your ticket?
Yero: In the playground.
Dina: Sorry … What are you saying?
Yero: She's looking for it in the … yippee!
Dina: Why are you cheering?
Yero: Olga has the bus ticket! It was under my sister's books.

b Read the dialogue again. Match the questions to the answers.

1 What is Olga doing?
2 Where is she looking for it?
3 Why is Yero cheering?

A She's looking for it in the playground.
B Because Olga has the bus ticket.
C She's looking for Yero's bus ticket.

c Read the boxes. Then mark in the dialogue in 3a:
questions with question words or without question words.

Am I Are you Is he/she/it Are we Are you Are they	helping? waiting?

Yes,	I am. we/you/they are. he/she/it is.
No,	I'm not. we/you/they aren't. he/she/it isn't.

Questions with question words:
Who is helping you?
What are you doing?
Where is she looking?
Why are you cheering?

4 Present progressive or simple present?

a Read the box and sentences.

1 Olga usually **eats** one sandwich for lunch.
2 Now Olga **is eating** two sandwiches.
3 Yero usually **drinks** water.
4 Today Yero **is drinking** tea.

Use the simple present to say what somebody usually does. → Module 2, p. 18 (simple present)

Use the present progressive to say what somebody is doing now or only today.

b Read the sentences again. Number the pictures (1–4).

1 

Means of transport:
(to) walk
(to) go by …
bike
car
bus
train
scooter

1 Means of transport

55 Listen and read. Number the pictures (1–6).

1 walk
2 go by bike / take your bike
3 go by car / take your car
4 go by train / take the train
5 go by bus / take the bus
6 go by scooter / take your scooter

Simple present and present progressive

Mon	Tues	Wed	Fri	Sat	Sun
✓	✓	✓	✓		

Olga usually **goes** to school by bus.
→ usually + simple present

Mon	Tues	Wed	Fri	Sat	Sun
		✓			

Today she**'s going** by bike.
→ today/now + present progressive

English and German
She's talking.
Sie spricht gerade.

2 How are they getting around today?

a Look at the pictures. Complete the sentences with the simple present or the present progressive.

1 Olga usually goes (go) by bus. But today she's going (go) by bike.
2 Mr Chan usually ____________ (take) the train.
But today he's ____________ (take) his car.
3 Yero and his sister usually ____________ (walk) home.
But today they ____________ (go) by bus.
4 Mrs Kern usually ____________ (go) by bike.
But today she ____________ (go) by scooter.
5 Mo usually ____________ (walk). But today he ____________ (take) his bike.
6 Jill and her friend usually ____________ (go) by bike.
But today they ____________ (walk).

→ My Words, pp. 66–67

b Mark the simple present and present progressive forms.

3 Places in town

Places in town:
bike shop
mobile phone shop
shopping centre
cafe
supermarket
hairdresser's

a 🔊56 Listen and read. Listen again and repeat.

a bike shop

a hairdresser's

a supermarket

a shopping centre

a mobile phone shop

a cafe

b Look at the map and number the places (1–9).

- ☐ a cafe
- ☐ a bike shop
- ☐ a bus stop
- ☐ Jill's flat
- ☐ a hairdresser's
- ☐ a mobile phone shop
- ☐ a park
- ☐ a shopping centre
- ☐ a supermarket

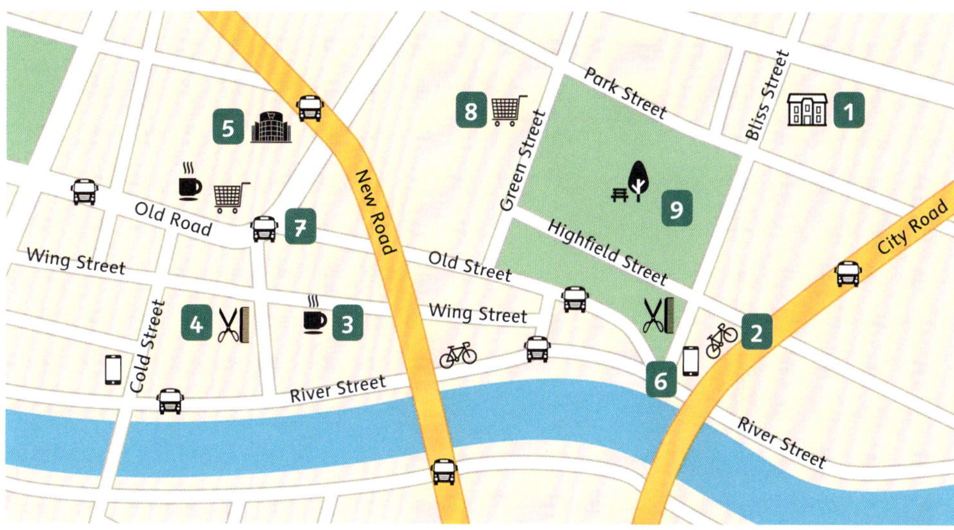

c 🔊57 Where are these places? Read the sentences and look at the map. Then listen and mark the right words.

1 Jill's flat is **near/in** the park.
2 The bike shop is **next to/behind** the mobile phone shop.
3 The cafe is **in/at** Wing Street.
4 The shopping centre is **to/on** New Road.
5 The bus stop is **at/in front of** the supermarket.
6 The hairdresser's is **next to/near** the cafe.

English and German
Jill's flat
Jills Wohnung

in the street
on the road
in front of
near
next to
opposite

d Choose a place on the map and say where it is. Can your partner say what the place is?

A: It's on Old Road and next to a cafe.
B: Is it a supermarket?
A: That's right./Sorry, that's wrong.

→ My Words, pp. 66–67

Asking and telling the way:
How can you get from … to …?
Go along the street.
Turn right.
Turn left.
The … is on the right/left.

4 Getting around Jill's hometown

a 58 Look and listen. Listen again and repeat.

Go along New Road.

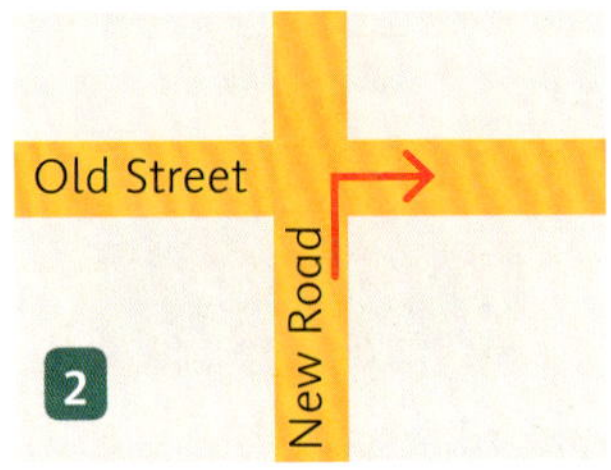

Turn right into Old Street.

The cafe is on the left.

b 59 Listen and read. Can you see the bike shop on the map?

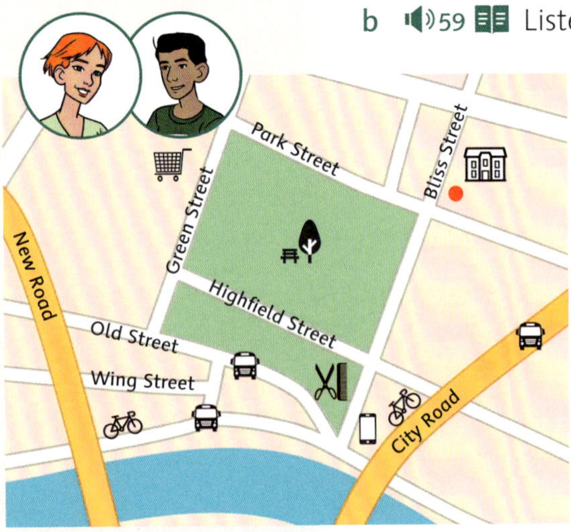

Jill: Look, Mo. This is a map of my hometown. My flat is in Bliss Street. That's near the park.
Mo: Cool. Let's see … I'm looking for a bike shop.
Jill: There's a bike shop on City Road.
Mo: How can you get from your flat to the bike shop?
Jill: Turn left and go along Bliss Street. Turn left into Highfield Street. Go along the street. Then turn right into City Road.
Mo: I can see the bike shop. It's on the right. And what about a supermarket and a hairdresser's?

c Describe the way from Jill's flat to the next supermarket (**1**) and to the hairdresser's (**2**) at the park.

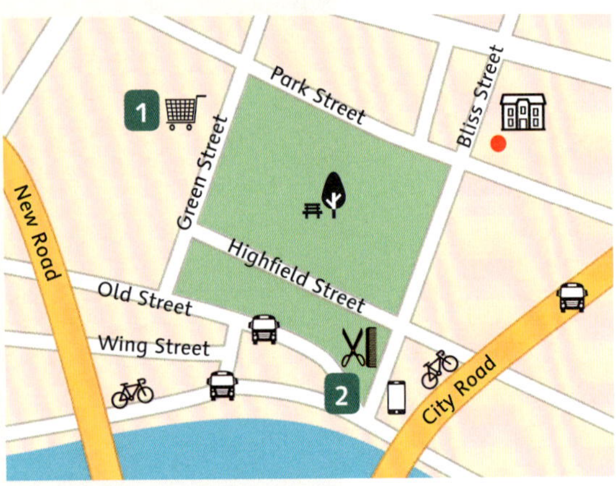

1 Turn left and go ________ Bliss Street. Turn ________ into Park Street and ________ into Green Street. The supermarket is on the ________.

2 Turn ________ and go along Bliss Street. Turn ________ into Highfield Street. The hairdresser's is on the ________.

5 Thinking about languages

Make a picture dictionary or a poster about places in your town. Write the places in English, German and your language(s).

supermarket
Supermarkt
супермáркет
سوبر ماركت

→ My Words, pp. 66–67

6 Helping a tourist in your town

a Read the text and look at the map.

Two classmates, a girl and a boy, are standing in front of your school. A tourist asks them the way.

Excuse me, please.
girl
boy
tourist

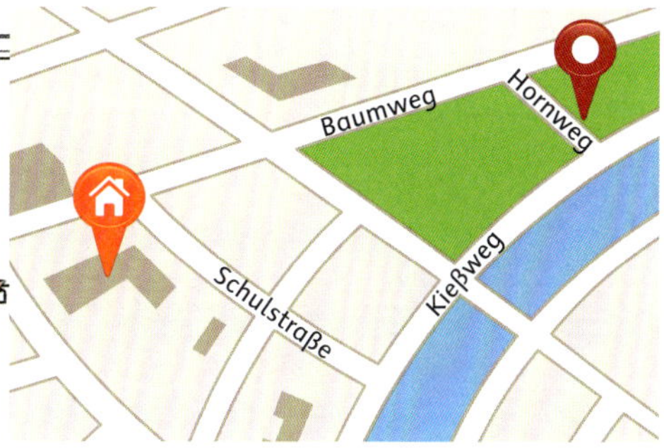

b 60 Listen to the dialogue. Who is right? Tick.

☐ the girl ☐ the boy ☐ the girl and the boy ☐ no one

c Use a map of your town.
Make dialogues and act them out with a partner:

A: Excuse me, please. How can I get from the school to …?
B: Turn … and go along … Turn into … The … is on the …
A: Thank you.
B: You're welcome.

the next bus stop • a hairdresser's • the park • *…straße* • a supermarket • *…weg* • …

TIP: You can use a free online map of your town.

TIP: It can be helpful to spell out proper names like *Wilhelm-straße*. For the letter *ß* say 'double s'. For *ä*, *ö*, *ü* say 'a (o, u) with two dots'.
→ Module 2, p. 24 (spelling words)

7 Telling the way at your school

a Draw a map of your school. Mark the main entrance.

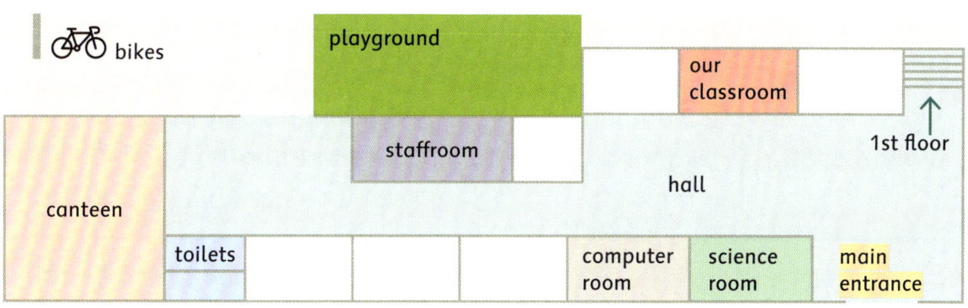

b Make dialogues and act them out with a partner.

A: Excuse me. I'm looking for the staffroom. How can I get there?
B: Turn left and go along the hall. The staffroom is on the right.
A: Thank you.
B: You're welcome.

our classroom • the canteen • the computer room • the science room • the toilets • …

Thank you.
You're welcome.

→ My Words, pp. 66–67

TIP: Describe pictures like this:
1. Say where people and objects are:
   I can see a woman on the right.
   There's a man on the right.
   There are five people on the left.
2. Say what people are doing:
   Dina **is** eat**ing**.
   Yero and Mo **are** play**ing** football.

1 Describing pictures

a What can you see the picture? Write in your exercise book.

I can see Mo, Nico, ... I can also see a bus stop, ...

b Compare with a partner.

c Match the sentences.

I can see a woman.
There's a man.
There are five people.

1 I can see Olga. — B

2 I can see Dina.

3 I can see Yero's bus ticket.

4 There's a mobile phone shop.

5 There are Mo and Nico.

6 There's a woman.

A It's between the cafe and the shoe shop.

B She's in front of Dina.

C They're in front of the shoe shop.

D She's next to the bus stop.

E She's behind Olga.

F It's under his shoe.

under ↔ on
in front of ↔ behind
in the middle
on the left
on the right
between ... and ...
shoe shop

d Write five sentences in your exercise book.

On the left In the middle On the right	Mo and Nico Yero a woman Dina and Olga a man	is are	looking for his bus ticket. standing in the queue. talking to each other. waiting for the bus. buying a mobile phone.

On the right Mo and Nico are ...

2 Describe your picture

a Draw a picture like.

b Don't show your picture to your partner, but describe it. Can your partner draw a sketch of your picture?

your picture

your partner's sketch

→ My Words, pp. 66–67

1 Write the transport phrases.

1 ______________ 3 ______________ 5 ______________

2 ______________ 4 ______________ 6 ______________

2 61 Look and listen. Is the information right or wrong? Tick.

1 The information is … ◯ right. ◯ wrong.

2 The information is … ◯ right. ◯ wrong.

3 The information is … ◯ right. ◯ wrong.

3 Describe the way from the cafe to the park in 2.

Turn right and go along ______________

____

____

4 Complete the sentences with the present progressive.

Yero and his little sister are in the park. Yero ______________ **(chat)** with his friends. And he ______________ **(look for)** his bus ticket. Yero's sister ______________ **(not look for)** the bus ticket. She ______________ **(play)**. Are his friends ______________ **(help)** him? Yes, they ______________ **(be)**. Dina and Olga ______________ **(help)**. But Mo and Nico ______________ **(not help)**. They ______________ **(go)** to the cinema. Yero's bus ticket ______________ **(lie)** under his little sister's books!

5 Present progressive or simple present? Mark the right verb form.

Selma usually **is having / has** fun at home. She always **is playing / plays** with her sisters. They often **are playing / play** hairdresser. They often **study / are studying** English together. But not today! Selma's sister **is going / goes** to the hospital today. Selma **is lying / lies** on the couch now. She **is thinking / thinks** about her sister: Good luck, Sister!

English	German	My notes
What are you doing?	Was machst du (gerade)? / Was macht ihr (gerade)?	
I'm lying in the park.	Ich liege (gerade) im Park.	
I'm looking for my bus ticket.	Ich suche (gerade) meine Busfahrkarte.	
Are you having fun? Yes, I am. / No, I'm not. Yes, we are. / No, we aren't.	Hast du (gerade) Spaß? / Habt ihr (gerade) Spaß? Ja. / Nein.	
(right) now	jetzt (gerade)	
at the moment	im Moment, im Augenblick	
today	heute	
Getting around town:	**Sich in der Stadt bewegen:**	
(to) wait for the bus	auf den Bus warten	
(to) go to the park	in den Park gehen	
(to) sit at the bus stop	an der Bushaltestelle sitzen	
(to) lie in the park	im Park liegen	
(to) stand in the queue	anstehen, Schlange stehen	
(to) buy snacks	Snacks kaufen	
(to) help sb.	jm. helfen	
(to) come	kommen	
(to) drink water	Wasser trinken	
(to) eat a sandwich	ein belegtes Brot essen	

Places in town (Orte in der Stadt)
cafe das Café • **cinema** das Kino • **bike shop** der Fahrradladen • **bus stop** die Bushaltestelle • **hairdresser's** der Friseurladen • **Jill's flat** Jills Wohnung • **mobile phone shop** der Handyladen • **park** der Park • **shoe shop** der Schuhladen • **shopping centre** das Einkaufszentrum • **supermarket** der Supermarkt

English	German	My notes
boy girl	der Junge das Mädchen	
tourist	der Tourist / die Touristin	

English	German	My notes
(to) talk to each other	miteinander sprechen	
(to) get ready for school	sich für die Schule fertig machen	

Means of transport (**Verkehrsmittel**)
(to) walk gehen • **(to) go by bike** Fahrrad fahren •
(to) go by car Auto fahren • **(to) go by bus** Bus fahren •
(to) go by train Zug fahren • **(to) go by scooter** Roller fahren

Asking and telling the way:	**Nach dem Weg fragen und den Weg beschreiben:**	
Excuse me, please.	Entschuldige bitte./ Entschuldigen Sie bitte.	
How can you get from ... to ...?	Wie kommt man von ... zu/nach ...?	
Thank you. You're welcome.	Danke. Gern geschehen.	
Go along the street.	Gehe die Straße entlang./ Gehen Sie ...	
Turn right./Turn left.	Biege rechts/links ab./ Biegen Sie rechts/links ab.	
on the road **in** the street	auf der Straße	
Describing pictures:	**Bilder beschreiben:**	
I can see a woman.	Ich sehe eine Frau.	
There's a man. **There are** five people.	Da ist ein Mann. Da sind fünf Personen.	
in the middle	in der Mitte	
on the left ↔ on the right	links ↔ rechts	
in front of ↔ behind	vor ↔ hinter	
on ↔ under	auf ↔ unter	
next to	neben	
near	in der Nähe von	
between ... and ...	zwischen ... und ...	

6 Planning a fashion show

What outfits are you going to present?

Our group is going to present beautiful dresses.

I'm going to make it shorter.

(to) plan a fashion show

(to) use sth.

(to) sew sth. on sth.

We're going to present the coolest T-shirts in the world.

We're going to wear disco outfits.

Are you going to buy all these clothes?

No, we aren't.

Clothes:
dress
trousers *(pl)*
T-shirt
shirt
sunglasses *(pl)*
shoe

Adjectives:
boring
beautiful ↔ ugly
cheap ↔ expensive
old ↔ new
big ↔ small
long ↔ short
colourful
cool
free
funny
second-hand

(to) send sth.

→ My Words, pp. 78–79

1 Planning a fashion show

62 Listen to and read the dialogues on page 68. Tick.

		right	wrong
1	The class is going to have a fashion show.	▢	▢
2	Olga and Maria are going to use new clothes.	▢	▢
3	Yero's group is going to have the most expensive outfits.	▢	▢
4	Jill's dad is going to send some second-hand clothes.	▢	▢

TIP:
1. Read the sentences.
2. Listen to or read the dialogues again.
3. Tick the right answers.
4. Check your answers.

2 What are they going to use?

a 63 Look at the pictures. Write *Y* for Yero, *O* for Olga and *M* for Mo. Listen and check your answers.

buttons

shoes

a shirt

a dress

paint

sunglasses

a T-shirt

trousers

Clothes and fashion:
button
paint
dress
trousers *(pl)*
shirt
T-shirt
shoe
sunglasses *(pl)*

is* or *looks
The T-shirt **is** new.
The T-shirt **looks** new.

b 64 Listen and read. Match the sentence parts.

1 The T-shirt is …
2 The trousers are …
3 The sunglasses look …
4 The shirt looks …

A very cool.
B boring.
C too long.
D new.

boring

very* and *too

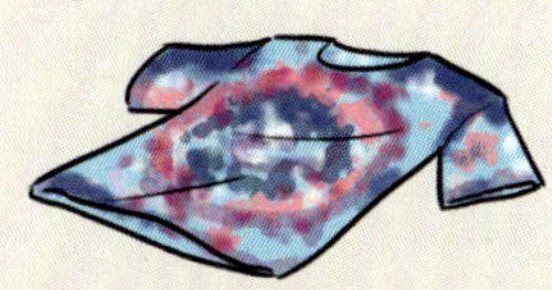
The T-shirt is **very colourful**.

The shirt is **too big**.

3 What do you think?

Write four or more sentences in your exercise book.

I think the	dress • paint • T-shirt	is looks	very too	big • boring • cool • cheap • colourful • beautiful • small • ugly • expensive • …
	buttons • shoes • sunglasses • trousers	are look		

I think the dress is too colourful and the trousers are …

→ My Words, pp. 78–79

1 The *going to*-future: positive and negative statements

Read the boxes. Complete the sentences with the *going to*-future.

I'm (= am) You're (=are) He/She/It's (= is) We're You're They're	going to	help them. buy it. make it.

I'm not You aren't He/She/It isn't We aren't You aren't They aren't	going to	help them. buy it. make it.

You form the *going to*-future with (not) am/are/is going to and the infinitive of the verb:
Yero's going to ask his mum for help.
We're not going to buy all these clothes.

You use going to to talk about intentions or plans for the future:
The groups are going to present their outfits at the fashion show in three weeks.

1 Mo's group *is going to present* **(present)** fashion of the 70s.
2 The students ______ **(wear)** cool outfits.
3 They ______ **(not wear)** hippie clothes.
4 They ______ **(dress)** like 70s disco dancers.
5 The group ______ **(not buy)** all clothes.
6 Jill's dad ______ **(send)** some second-hand clothes.

2 The *going to*-future: questions and short answers

Read the boxes. Then match the questions to the answers.

Am I Are you Is he/she/it Are we Are you Are they	going to	help me? buy it? make it?

Yes,	I am. we/you/they are. he/she/it is.
No,	I'm not. we/you/they aren't. he/she/it isn't.

Questions with question words
What are you going to present?
How are you going to do this?
Who is going to help you?
→ Module 3, p. 33 (question words)

1 What are you going to present?
2 Are you going to buy T-shirts?
3 Is Mr Chan going to help you?
4 Who is going to help you?

A No, we aren't. They're free.
B The coolest and cheapest T-shirts!
C My mum.
D No he isn't.

3 The comparison of adjectives: -er/-est, more/most

a Read the boxes.

Adjectives (like *good*, *beautiful*, *old*) say how people or things are or what they look like.

Adjectives can go before nouns or after verbs like *be* or *look*:

This is a beautiful dress. This dress looks beautiful.

b Read the box. Complete the table with the right adjective forms.

Basic form:

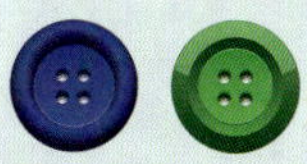

The blue button is as big as the green button.

Comparative with -er:

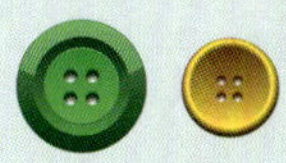

The green button is bigger than the yellow button.

Superlative with -est:

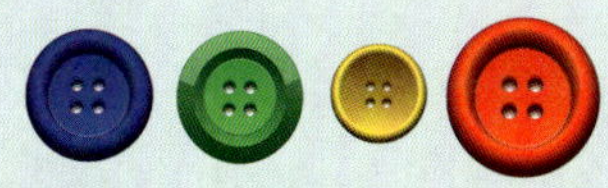

The red button is the biggest.

You use -er/-est with one-syllable adjectives: cool → cooler, coolest
You also use -er/-est with two-syllable adjectives ending in -y: fun·ny → funnier, funniest

basic form	comparative	superlative
cool	____________	____________
old	____________	____________
big	bigger	____________
ugly	uglier	____________

c Read the box and complete the table.

Some adjectives have two or more syllables: bo·ring, ex·pen·sive, beau·ti·ful

With these adjectives you use more and most:
A T-shirt is more expensive than a button.
This is the most expensive T-shirt in the shop.

basic form	comparative	superlative
expensive	more expensive	most expensive
beautiful	more beautiful	____________
boring	____________	____________

d 65 Read the box. Listen and repeat.

Some adjectives have irregular comparison forms, for example:
good: better, best bad: worse, worst much, many: more, most

Clothes:
jacket
pullover
skirt
sock
jeans (*pl*)
boot
trainer

1 Talking about clothes

a 66 Look at the pictures. Then listen, read and repeat.

b 67 What do Olga and Yero say about the clothes? Listen and number the adjectives (1–8).

1 
a sweatshirt

2 
jeans

3 
boots

4 
a jacket

5 
a skirt

6 
trainers

7 
socks

8 
a pullover

(2) cool	( ) boring	( ) good	( ) expensive
( ) beautiful	( ) colourful	( ) funny	( ) ugly

c Mark the adjectives in 1b: comparative and superlative with -er and -est, with *more and most* or irregular. Look at page 71 for help.

d Compare the clothes. Write six or more sentences in your exercise book.

The	sweatshirt • skirt • jacket • pullover	looks	...-er than	the	boots • skirt • jacket • jeans • pullover • ...
	jeans • boots • socks • trainers	look	more ... than		

The trainers look better than the boots.

e Talk to a partner.

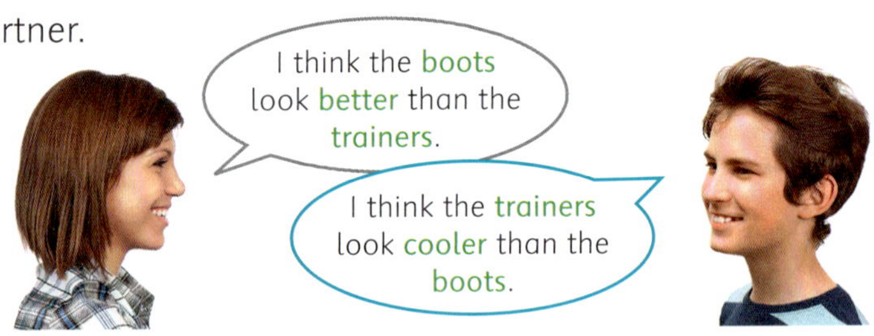

TIP: There are free online dictionaries for most languages. You can also use the online English-German dictionary for this workbook.

2 Thinking about languages

Look up these clothes words in a dictionary – German and your languages. Are they similar or different? Talk in a group.

pullover

T-shirt

blouse

jeans

top

sweatshirt

→ My Words, pp. 78–79

3 Clothes and money

> **TIP:** When you listen, you don't need to understand every word.

a 🔊68 Look at the picture and listen. Tick the right answers.

- ☐ The clothes are all second hand.
- ☐ The shoes were more expensive than the jacket.
- ☐ Jill's dad is going to come to the fashion show.
- ☐ Jill is going to send her dad photos of the fashion show.

all (the) clothes

money
pound
penny, *pl* pence

b 🔊69 How much were these clothes? Listen and write.

1 The shirt was £2 ______.
2 The jeans were ______.
3 The jacket was ______.
4 The T-shirt was ______.
5 The shoes were ______.
6 The sunglasses were ______.

British money

You write	You say
1p	one p [pi:]
20p	twenty p
£1.50	one fifty
£5	five pounds
£10.90	ten ninety

How much is the shirt?
The shirt is £2.
How much are the shoes?
The shoes are £10.

c Check the sentences from 3b. What's <u>the most expensive</u> or <u>the cheapest</u> piece of clothing? Complete the sentences.

1 cheap: T-shirt, shoes or shirt?
The T-shirt is the ______ piece of clothing.

2 expensive: shirt, shoes or jeans?
The ______ piece of clothing.

3 cheap: T-shirt, jeans or sunglasses?
The ______ piece of clothing.

Clothes
The word clothes has no singular form and you can't count it:

clothes *(pl)*

a piece of clothing *(sg)*

two pieces of clothing *(pl)*

4 Thinking about cultures

Britain has pounds and pence. What about Germany and other countries? Make a poster about money in different countries.

(to) ask sb. for sth.
(to) phone sb.
(to) cut sth.
(to) work on a project
sewing tools *(pl)*

5 What are Olga's plans for this week?

70 Look, listen and read. Complete the sentences with the *going to*-future.

English and German
Yero **is going to** ask his mum for help.
Yero **wird/will** seine Mutter um Hilfe **bitten**.

1 Olga ______________________ on Monday.
2 She ______________________ on Tuesday.
3 She ______________________ on Wednesday.
4 She ______________________ on Thursday.
5 She ______________________ on Friday.
6 She ______________________ on Saturday and Sunday.

6 Your plans for the weekend

a Write three sentences about your plans for Saturday and Sunday.

do my homework • go to the gym • go swimming • go to the youth club • meet my friends • visit my grandma/aunt/… • watch TV • …

I'm going to ______________________

____

____

b Talk to two or more partners. Do they have the same plans?

TIP: Change the green words in the dialogue:
I'm going to go to the youth club on Saturday.
→ *I'm going to meet my friends on Saturday.*

What about you?
Me too.

→ My Words, pp. 78–79

7 Plan your own fashion project and present it

a 71 Listen, read and look. Number the texts (1–4).

Finally, I'm going to sew the shirt and the T-shirt together.
My friend Leila ist going to help me. ☐

Today I'm going to present my fashion project 'T-blouse'.
I'm going to use an old T-shirt, one of my dad's old shirts and some sewing tools. ☐

First I'm going to cut off the upper part and the cuffs of the shirt. Then I'm going to cut off the lower part of the T-shirt. ☐

In this picture you can see my new 'T-blouse'. I like it because looks beautiful. And it's unique – nobody has a blouse like this! ☐

Giving a short talk:
Today I'm going to talk about …

First …

Then …

Finally, …

That's the end of my presentation.

Thank you for listening.

Do you have any questions?

b Make notes for your presentation.

TIP: Look up more words in an online dictionary.

1 Today I'm going to present my fashion project '…'

2 I'm going to use … old shoes • paint • my dad's old hat • second-hand clothes • sewing tools • …

3 First I'm going to … Then I'm going to … Finally, I'm going to … get • cut (off) • draw • buy • sew • …

4 In this picture you can see my new '…' I like it because it's beautiful • very cheap • cool • …

5 That's the end of my presentation. Thank you for listening. Do you have any questions?

1. What fashion project are you going to present?
2. What are you going to use?
3. How are you going to make it?
4. What is special about your new outfit? Why do you like it?
5. End your presentation.

c Present your project in a group.

→ My Words, pp. 78–79

1 How to plan and give a short talk

traditional costume

a Prepare a short talk about fashion: your favourite outfit, a celebrity's outfit or a traditional costume. Collect your ideas in this mind map:

TIP: Look at pages 69, 72 and 75 for more words and phrases. Look up more words in an online dictionary.
→ M2, p. 26 (Online dictionaries and apps)

My pictures

____

____

____

What does it look like?

It's ______________________

____

It has ______________________

Fashion: ______________________

When do you wear it?

People wear it ______________________

____

____

Why do I like it?

Because ______________________

____

____

TIP: How to plan and give a short talk:
1. Collect ideas in a mind map, in a list or on cards.
2. Plan your talk and write down typical phrases.
3. Practise your talk alone or with a partner.
4. Give your talk in a group or in class.

Today I'm going to talk about ...
Now I'm going to tell you ...
That's the end of my talk.

b Read the phrases for a short talk. Number the phrases (1–7).

- ◯ Do you have any questions?
- ◯ Finally, I'm going tell you ...
- ◯ First I'm going to show you some pictures.
- ◯ Thank you for listening.
- (1) Today I'm going to talk about ...
- ◯ Now I'm going to tell you ...
- ◯ That's the end of my talk.

TIP: Listen again to Olga's talk. You can use her phrases. Change her ideas for your own ideas.

c 72 Listen to Olga's short talk and check your answers. Copy the phrases 1–6 in your exercise book.

d 72 Listen again. Make notes on cards. Use your ideas from 1a and the phrases from 1b.

e Practise your talk alone or with a partner.

f Give your talk in a group.

→ My Words, pp. 78–79

1 73 Listen and tick the clothes that Jill is going to buy.

2 Complete the sentences with the *going to*-future.

1 Jill ____________________ a rugby match.

2 She ____________________ to the cinema.

3 She ____________________ a new dress.

4 She ____________________ her dad.

Plans for the weekend:
- watch rugby match ✓
- go to cinema ✗
- buy new dress ✗
- phone Dad ✓

3 Complete the sentences with the right forms of the adjectives.

The red skirt is __________ than the pink skirt.

The blue skirt is the __________.

The brown jacket is __________ than the blue jacket.

The black jacket is the __________.

The pink socks are __________ than the yellow socks.

The green socks are the __________.

4 What's the right order? Number the phrases.

☐ Do you have any questions?

☐ First I'm going to show you some pictures.

☐ Finally, I'm going tell you why I like my outfit.

☐ That's the end of my talk.

☐ Today I'm going to talk about my favourite outfit.

☐ Thank you for listening.

☐ Now I'm going to tell you what my outfit looks like.

English	German	My notes
What outfits are you going to present?	Welche Outfits werdet/wollt ihr präsentieren?	
Our group is going to present beautiful dresses.	Unsere Gruppe wird/will schöne Kleider präsentieren.	
I'm going to make the dress shorter.	Ich werde/will das Kleid kürzer machen.	
We're going to present the coolest T-shirts in the world.	Wir werden/wollen die coolsten T-Shirts der Welt präsentieren.	
We're going to wear disco outfits.	Wir werden/wollen Disco-Kleidung tragen.	
Are you going to buy all these clothes? No, we aren't./Yes, we are.	Werdet/Wollt ihr all diese Kleider kaufen? Nein./Ja.	
(to) plan a fashion show	eine Modenschau planen	
(to) use sth. (for sth.)	etw. (für etw.) benutzen	
(to) sew sth. on sth.	etw. an etw. nähen	

Clothes and fashion (Kleidung und Mode)
boot der Stiefel • **button** der Knopf • **costume** das Kostüm, die Verkleidung • **dress** das Kleid • **paint** die (Textil-)Farbe • **pullover** der Pullover • **sewing tools** *(pl)* das Nähzeug • **shirt** das Hemd • **skirt** der Rock • **shoe** der Schuh • **sock** die Socke • **sunglasses** *(pl)* die Sonnenbrille • **jacket** die Jacke • **trainer** der Turnschuh • **trousers** *(pl)* die Hose • **T-shirt** das T-Shirt

The T-shirt is **very** colourful.	Das T-Shirt ist sehr bunt.
The shirt is **too** big.	Das Hemd ist zu groß.
The T-shirt **is** new. The T-shirt **looks** new.	Das T-Shirt ist neu. Das T-Shirt sieht neu aus.

Adjectives (Adjektive)
beautiful (wunder)schön • **big** groß • **boring** langweilig • **cheap** billig • **colourful** bunt, farbig • **cool** cool • **expensive** teuer • **free** kostenlos; frei • **funny** lustig • **long** lang • **new** neu • **old** alt • **second-hand** aus zweiter Hand, gebraucht • **small** klein • **short** kurz • **traditional** traditionell • **ugly** hässlich

English	German	My notes
good, better, the best	gut, besser, der/die/das beste	
bad, worse, the worst	schlecht, schlecher, der/die/das schlechteste	
much/many, more, the most	viel, mehr, der/die/das meiste	
clothes *(pl)*	die Kleidung, die Kleidungsstücke *(Pl.)*	
clothing a piece of clothing	die Kleidung das Kleidungsstück	
money	das Geld	
pound (£) penny, *pl* pence (pennies)	das Pfund *(britische Währung)* der Penny	
How much is the shirt? The shirt is £2. How much are the shoes? The shoes are £10.	Wieviel kostet das Hemd? Das Hemd kostet 2 Pfund. Wieviel kosten die Schuhe? Die Schuhe kosten 10 Pfund.	
What about you?	Und du? / Und Sie?	
Me too.	Ich auch.	
(to) ask sb. for sth. (to) ask sb. for help	jn. um etwas bitten jn. um Hilfe bitten	
(to) phone sb.	jn. anrufen	
(to) cut sth.	etwas schneiden, abschneiden	
(to) work on a project	an einem Projekt arbeiten	
Giving a short talk:	**Einen Kurzvortrag halten:**	
Today I'm going to present/ talk about …	Heute präsentiere/ spreche ich über …	
First I'm going to show you some pictures.	Zuerst werde ich euch ein paar Bilder zeigen.	
Finally,/Now I'm going to tell you …	Zuletzt/Jetzt werde ich euch sagen …	
That's the end of my talk/ presentation.	Das war mein Vortrag/ meine Präsentation.	
Thank you for listening.	Danke für's Zuhören.	
Do you have any questions?	Habt ihr noch Fragen?	

7 International food buffet

international food buffet

We've made the fruit salad.

Have you cut the bread yet?

No, I haven't./Yes, I have.

But I've just cut the vegetables.

What have you done so far?

(to) bake
(to) clean
(to) cook
(to) try

(to) do,
past participle: done

(to) drink,
past participle: drunk

(to) eat,
past participle: eaten

(to) make,
past participle: made

(to) put,
past participle: put

(to) see,
past participle: seen

I've never seen so much food.

Have you ever eaten tabouleh before?

Food:
bread
fruit
cake
salad
soup
olive

Drink:
tea
juice
water
milk

cold
delicious
yummy *(infml)*

→ My Words, pp. 92–93

1 Is everything ready for the international food buffet?

a 74 Look at page 80. Listen and read.
b Who has done what? Read again. Match the sentence parts.
c Number the pictures (1–5).

1 Yero and Maria
2 Mo
3 Olga
4 Pablo

A has just cut the vegetables. **(1)**
B has already cleaned the table. **(2)**
C has eaten all the tabouleh. **(3)**
D have already made the fruit salad. **(4)**
E hasn't cut the bread yet. **(5)**

2 Fruit and vegetables

a Read and write the words from the box in the food network.

~~apple~~ • banana • bell pepper • ~~carrot~~ • cucumber • lemon • orange • strawberry • tomato

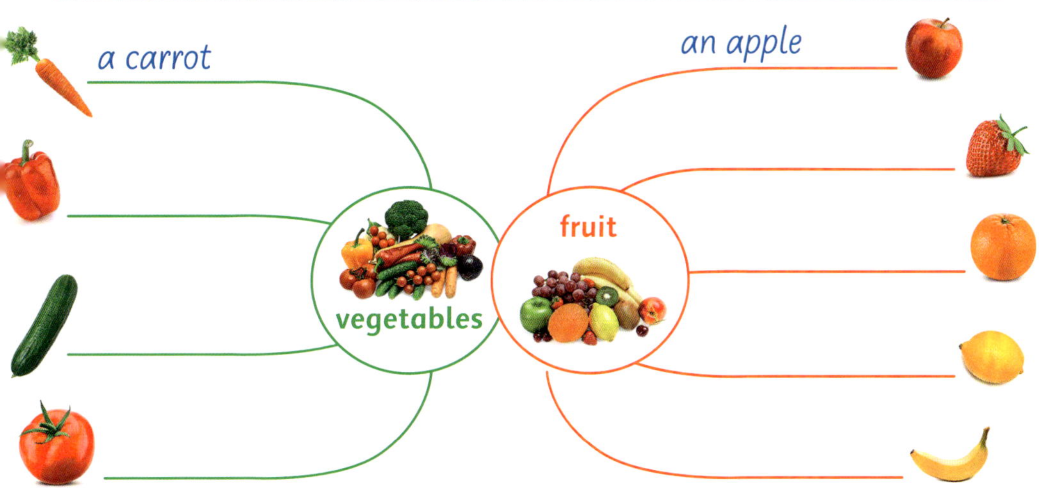

Fruit and vegetables:
- apple
- banana
- bell pepper
- carrot
- cucumber
- lemon
- orange
- strawberry, *pl* strawberries
- tomato, *pl* tomatoes

***a* or *an*?**
Check how you **say** the next word:
a carrot
an apple

With **A**, **E**, **I**, **O**, **U** you say **an**.

→ Sounds, p. 110

b 75 Listen and check.
c What have you eaten this week? Complete the sentence with two vegetables or fruits.

I've eaten some ______________________________

d Compare with a partner. Has he or she eaten the same food?

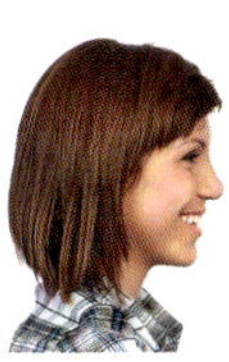

I've eaten some strawberries and tomatoes this week. What about you?

I haven't eaten any strawberries this week. But I've eaten some tomatoes and bananas.

I've eaten some ...
I haven't eaten any ...

→ My Words, pp. 92–93

1 The present perfect: positive statements

a Read the boxes. Then complete the sentences with regular present perfect forms. Match sentences 1–3 to sentences A–C.

I've (= have) You've He/She/It's (= has) We've You've They've	baked. cleaned. cooked.

You form the present perfect of regular verbs with have/has and the past participle with -ed.
⚠ Be careful with the spelling of these verbs:
bake: baked
stop: stopped
try: tried (but: play – played)

I've cleaned the table. Now we can put the drinks on it.
Jill has cooked tomato soup. It looks yummy!

You use the present perfect to say that something has or hasn't happened at some time in the past. There's often an effect on the present.

1 The students ____________ **(clean)** all the tables.
2 Mr Chan ____________ **(try)** the Jollof rice.
3 Yero ____________ **(finish)** all his tasks.

A But it's too spicy for him.
B Now he's tired, but happy.
C Now people can eat there.

b Read the box. Complete the table with irregular past participle forms from page 80.

I've (= have) You've He/She/It's (= has) We've You've They've	eaten vegetables. drunk water. been very nice.

You form the present perfect of irregular verbs with have/has and the past participle of the verb. There is no rule for the past participle of irregular verbs. You need to learn them.

→ Irregular verbs, pp. 108–109

infinitive	simple past	past participle
be	was / were	been
have	had	had
do	did	____________
cut	cut	____________
drink	drank	____________
eat	ate	____________
make	made	____________
see	saw	____________

c Complete the sentences with irregular present perfect forms.

1 I ____________ **(eat)** too much cake!
2 We ____________ **(do)** the shopping.
3 Mo ____________ **(cut)** the bread now.
4 Sina ____________ **(make)** a tomato salad.
5 She ____ never ____________ **(be)** to the canteen.
6 They ____________ **(have)** lots of fun so far.

2 The present perfect: negative statements

a Read the boxes. Then complete the sentences with *haven't* or *hasn't*. Match sentences 1–4 to sentences A–D.

I haven't	baked.
You haven't	cleaned.
He/She/It hasn't	cooked.
We haven't	eaten.
You haven't	drunk.
They haven't	

You make negative statements in the present perfect with haven't/hasn't and the past participle of the verb.

With negative statements in the present perfect, you often use yet or before.

1 The students __________ finished their project.
2 I __________ seen the film yet.
3 Yero __________ studied for the test yet.
4 You __________ done your homework yet.
5 Olga __________ eaten lasagne before.

A But she really likes it.
B So you can't go to the cinema.
C Have you seen it?
D They're still working on it.
E He's going to study at the weekend.

b Complete the sentences with the positive and negative forms of the present perfect. Be careful with the irregular verbs.

1 Jill *has been* to the supermarket.
But she __________ to the copy shop yet.
2 She __________ the chocolate cake.
But she __________ the lemon cake yet.
3 Pablo __________ carrot juice before.
But he __________ cucumber juice.
4 They __________ the tables.
But they __________ the chairs yet.

1

✓ be | not be ✗

2

✓ make | not make ✗

3

✓ try | not try ✗

4

✓ clean | not clean ✗

c What have or haven't you done this week? Write sentences.

1 (not) eat | enough fruit | enough vegetables
I've eaten __________
2 (not) do | all my homework | exercises
____
3 (not) use | a smartphone | a computer
____

3 The present perfect: questions and short answers

a Read the boxes. Then write the questions. Match the questions to the answers.

Have	I you we you they	eaten yet? helped you? been here?
Has	he/she/it	

Yes,	I you we/you/they	have.
No,		haven't.
Yes,	he/she/it	has.
No,		hasn't.

Questions with question words
What have you done?
Where has he been?
Who has cut the bread?

1 been | ~~Where~~ | you | have | ?
Where ____________________

2 the cake | haven't | cut | you | Why | yet | ?
____

3 you | tried | the food | Have | ?
____

4 seen | you | Jill's photos | Have | ?
____

A Because Jill wanted to cut it.

B No, I haven't. Jill is going to show them to me.

C I've been here in the canteen.

D Yes, I have. I've tried all the salads.

b 76 Listen to the dialogue and check your answers.

4 Signal words: adverbs of indefinite time

Read the box. Then mark the right answers.

I've already eaten.
We've just come home.
I've never eaten tabouleh before.
I've seen the film before.
Mo hasn't cut the bread yet.
Have you ever drunk tomato juice?
Have you cut the bread yet?

The present perfect tells you that something has or hasn't happened. You don't know when it happened.
With the present perfect you can only use adverbs of indefinite time like:

already	never	ever?
just	not ... yet	yet?
before	often	

1 Which two adverbs stand at the end of a sentence?

already • before • ever • just • never • often • yet

2 Which four adverbs aren't signal words for the present perfect?

already • an hour ago • ever • just • last week • never • on Monday • yesterday

5 Present perfect or simple past?

a Read the blue boxes.
Complete the sentences with
the verb forms from the green box.

I've baked a cake. You can try it now.

past → present

I baked it yesterday.
I used lots of chocolate.

past → present

You use the present perfect to say that something has happened in the past. It isn't important when it happened. You're thinking about the past and the present.
You often use signal words like *already, just, ever, never, yet, …*

You use the simple past to say when something happened in the past. You're only thinking about the past.
You often use signal words like *yesterday, in 2018, last week, ten minutes ago, …*

→ Module 4, p. 44

did … make | ~~'ve made~~ • tried | haven't tried • finished | Have … finished •
Did … clean | 've … cleaned

1 I've made ______ a chocolate cake for the buffet. – When ______ you ______ it?

2 I ______ the lemon cake yet, but I ______ the chocolate cake this morning.

3 ______ you ______ your homework yet? – Yes, I ______ it ten minutes ago.

4 ______ you ______ the table this morning? – No, but I ______ just ______ it.

b Read Mo's text and mark the right verb forms.

My first day at school in Germany
My first day at school in Germany **have been / was** after I moved here last summer. In Syria I **haven't gone / didn't go** to school for a year. Last summer I **have come / came** to Germany with my brother.
I like this school because most of the teachers and students are nice. I**'ve made / made** lots of new friends. Olga and Yero are my best friends in class. I**'ve learned / learned** a lot too. Mr Chan says that my German **has improved / improved** a lot. And Jill says that my English **has improved / improved** too. I usually don't study at the weekend. But last weekend I**'ve studied / studied** English with Olga and Yero. It **has been / was** fun!

c Write four or more sentences about yourself. You can use the text from 4b.
My first day at school in Germany was in August 2018 …

d Compare your sentences with a partner.

1 Dad's cooking

a 77 Jill's dad is in Germany for two weeks. He cooks for Jill every day. What has Jill eaten so far? Listen, read and tick.

☐ pasta with tomato sauce

☐ yoghurt

☐ cheese

☐ fish and chips

☐ vegetable curry

☐ meat

☐ potatoes

☐ biscuits

☐ cereal

b 77 What's Jill's favourite food and what is she allergic to? Listen again and write.

Jill's favourite food is ____________________

Jill is allergic to ____________________

c Look and read. Match the adjectives to the food.

salty | sweet | cold | spicy | hot

d 78 Listen and check.

2 Your food

a Copy and complete the mind map in your exercise book.

My food
- I like
- I don't like
- I haven't tried yet
- I'm allergic to

b Write five or more sentences in your exercise book.

I like sweet food: biscuits, cake and chocolate. I also like spicy food: ...

c Compare your sentences with a partner.

(to) cook

Food and meals:
cereal
biscuit
vegetable curry
fish and chips *(pl)*
meat
pasta with tomato sauce
yoghurt
cheese
potato, *pl* potatoes

English and German

E	G
biscuit	Keks
cake	Kuchen

Describing food:
sweet
spicy
salty
hot
cold
I'm allergic to ...

TIP: Look up more words in an online dictionary.

→ Module 2, p. 26 (Online dictionaries and apps)

→ My Words, pp. 92–93

3 A checklist for the buffet

a Write the present perfect forms of the verbs with *he*.

ask – *he has asked* clean – ______ write – ______

buy – ______ make – ______

> **TIP:** You can look up the irregular past participle forms on pages 108–109.

b Read Yero, Mo and Olga's checklists. What jobs have or haven't they done? Write in your exercise book.

Yero's jobs
- buy drinks ✓
- buy fruit ✗
- make puff-puffs ✗

Mo's jobs
- buy vegetables ✗
- make tabouleh ✗
- clean the room ✓

Olga's jobs
- write food signs ✓
- buy biscuits ✗
- clean the tables ✓

Yero has bought drinks and … He hasn't …

4 Your checklist for this week

a Choose four jobs from the box. Write them in a table in your exercise book.

buy new pens for school • clean my bike • do all my homework • practise my instrument • study for the test • write a message to my best friend

	Me	*Partner*
study for the test	✓	
do all my homework		
…		

b Tick the jobs that you have done already.

c Write down the present perfect forms of the verbs in your checklist.

clean – *I've cleaned* do – ______

study – ______ practise – ______

d Find a partner and talk about your jobs.

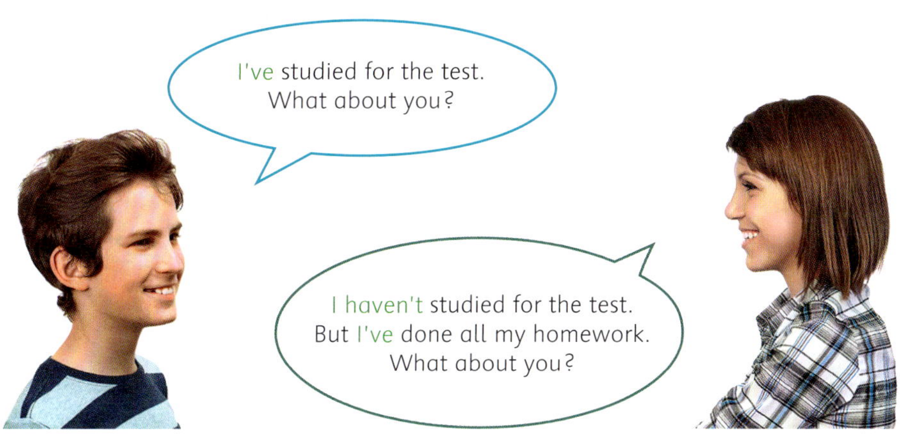

→ My Words, pp. 92–93

... is/are a drink/a food/
... that is ...
- spicy/sweet/...
- comes from ...
- you eat cold/drink hot/...
- filled with ...

5 Street food is international

a 79 Listen and read. Number the pictures (1–3).

1 Falafel are vegetable balls that come from Lebanon.
2 Ayran is a yoghurt drink that you drink cold.
3 Warga is a green tea that you drink sweet and very hot.

☐  ☐  ☐ 

b Write about three or more foods in your exercise book.

burritos • burgers • crepes • currywurst • kumpir • tacos • ...	is / are	a food • a drink • a pasta • ...	that	is very spicy/sweet/... comes from ... you eat/drink hot/... is filled with ...

Tacos are a traditional Mexican food that's filled with meat or vegetables.

c Find a partner who knows about other food.

6 A game

a Write five or more cards.
b Play a game in class:
- Play in teams.
- The quizmaster reads the cards out loud.
- The teams answer: "It's .../They're ..."
- The fastest team gets a point.

It's a drink that you can drink hot or cold. It's white.
(It's milk.)

They're vegetable balls that come from Lebanon.
(They're falafel.)

TIP: Do some research on the internet to find out more about your favourite food.

7 Thinking about cultures

a Make a poster about your favourite food or drink.
- What's your favourite food/drink?
- What is it? (pasta, meat, ...)
- Is it spicy, sweet, ...?
- Do you eat/drink it hot or cold?
- What country is it from?

b Walk around in class and look at the posters. Talk to different partners about their favourite food and drink.

MY FAVOURITE FOOD

My favourite food is pelmeni. It's pasta that's filled with meat. It's not very spicy. You eat it hot. It's from Russia.

→ My Words, pp. 92–93

8 Interview: Have you ever eaten goat cheese?

a Complete questions 1 and 2 with two more food words.
b Write three more questions. You can use questions from 8d.
c Answer the questions for your yourself (*Me*).

Questions	Me	Partner
1 Have you ever eaten …		
– *goat cheese?*		
–		
–		
2 Have you ever drunk …		
– *ayran?*		
–		
–		
3		
4		
5		

d Ask and answer your questions with a partner. Write down his or her answers in the table in 8c.

TIP: Change the green words and make your own sentences.

What's your favourite food?
My favourite food is pasta with tomato sauce.
Is it spicy/sweet/…?
It can be salty or spicy.
What have you eaten today?
I've eaten cereal with milk and a sandwich.
What did you eat yesterday?
I ate a sandwich, falafel, a salad and a yoghurt.
What food are you allergic to?
I'm not allergic to any kind of food.

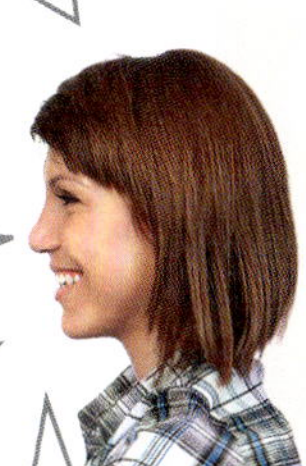

e Record or film your interview and present it to the class.

→ My Words, pp. 92–93

(to) forget, *past participle*: forgotten

TIP: How to understand listening texts:
1. Look at the pictures and read the heading.
2. Read the tasks and other information.
3. Listen and do the tasks (use a pencil).
4. Listen again and check. Correct your mistakes.
5. You don't need to understand every word.

1 How to understand listening texts

a Look at the picture. What do you think the dialogue will be about? Tick.

- ◯ Jill has forgotten to go shopping.
- ◯ Jill has forgotten to buy something.
- ◯ Jill can't read the shopping list.

b 80 Listen and check your answer in 1a. Were you right?

c 80 Read the sentences. Listen again and tick.

1 Jill is talking to …	◯ her father.	◯ her aunt.	◯ her mother.
2 Jill is in …	◯ Britain.	◯ Germany.	◯ Spain.
3 Jill didn't buy …	◯ potatoes.	◯ meat.	◯ milk.

2 More listening: At the fruit bar

TIP: You can listen to the text one, two or more times.

a Look at the poster. What fruit do you like?

b 81 Who chooses what? Listen. Listen again and tick (✓) or cross (✗).

	Olga	Mo	Yero
apples	✗		
bananas	✓		
lemons	✗		
oranges	✓		
strawberries	✓		

c 81 Why don't they eat some of the fruit? Listen again and make notes in your exercise book like this:

Olga: ✗ apples – allergic, ✗ lemons – doesn't like

d Write full answers in your exercise book. Use these phrases:

… doesn't eat	apples • bananas • lemons • oranges • strawberries	because	he/she's allergic to them. he/she doesn't like them.

Olga doesn't eat apples because she's allergic to them.
She doesn't eat lemons because she doesn't like them.

→ My Words, pp. 92–93

1 Write down the food words.

1 ____________
2 ____________
3 ____________
4 ____________
5 ____________

1 
2 
3 
4 
5 

2 What's the right word? Read and write.

1 It's a green vegetable that you eat cold. You can make salad with it.

It's ____________

2 It's a drink that you drink hot or cold. In England, people drink it a lot.

It's ____________

3 82 What has Mo done and what hasn't he done yet?

Listen and tick (✓) or cross (✗). Then write full sentences.

1 *Mo* ____________
2 *He* ____________
3 ____________
4 ____________

- ◯ buy the fruit
- ◯ cut the fruit
- ◯ make tabouleh
- ◯ clean the table

4 Write the questions in the present perfect.

you | (eat) | yet | the cake • what | (do) | you • (try) | ever | you | tomato salad

1 ____________ Yes, I have. It was really good!
2 ____________ I've cleaned the tables.
3 ____________ No, I haven't. I don't like tomatoes.

5 Read and mark the right verb form.

When Olga lived in Russia, she **has gone / went** to three different schools: When she was eight, her family **has moved / moved to** a small town. When she was ten, her family **has moved / moved** again. Last winter Olga **has come / came** to Germany with her dad. She **hasn't spoken / didn't speak** any German then. But she **has studied / studied** a lot and so her German **has improved / improved**. Her English **has improved / improved** too!

English	German	My notes
international food buffet	ein Büfett mit internationalen Gerichten	
We've made the fruit salad.	Wir haben den Obstsalat gemacht.	
Have you cut the bread yet?	Hast du schon das Brot geschnitten?	
No, I haven't. / Yes, I have.	Ja. / Nein.	
But I've just cut the vegetables.	Aber ich habe gerade das Gemüse geschnitten.	
I've already put tea on the table.	Ich habe schon Tee auf den Tisch gestellt.	
I've never seen so much food.	Ich habe noch nie so viel Essen gesehen.	
Have you ever eaten tabouleh before?	Hast du schon mal Tabouleh gegessen?	

Irregular past participles

be	was/were	been	sein; war; (ist) gewesen
cut	cut	cut	schneiden; schnitt; (hat) geschnitten
do	did	done	tun; tat; (hat) getan
drink	drank	drunk	trinken; trank; (hat) getrunken
eat	ate	eaten	essen; aß; (hat) gegessen
forget	forgot	forgotten	vergessen; vergaß; (hat) vergessen
go	went	gone	gehen; ging; (ist) gegangen
have	had	had	haben; hatte; (hat) gehabt
make	made	made	machen; machte; (hat) gemacht
put	put	put	legen; legte; (hat) gelegt
see	saw	seen	sehen; sah; (hat) gesehen

→ Irregular verbs, pp. 108–109

I**'ve** eaten **some** fruit.	Ich habe Obst gegessen.	
I **haven't** eaten **any** fruit.	Ich habe kein Obst gegessen.	
(to) bake	backen	
(to) clean	sauber machen, putzen	
(to) cook	kochen, *(Essen)* zubereiten	
(to) try	probieren, versuchen	

English	German	My notes
already • not … yet • yet? • never • ever? • just • before • so far		
Olga and Mo have **already** gone.	schon	
Olga has**n't** made the signs **yet**.	noch nicht	
Have you cut the vegetables **yet**?	schon	
I've **never** been to Britain.	noch nie	
Have you **ever** eaten fish?	schon mal	
I've **just** tried to phone her.	gerade (eben)	
I haven't eaten tabouleh **before**.	vorher	
I haven't seen Yero **so far**.	bis jetzt	
… is a drink/food/… that comes from/is filled with/…	… ist ein Getränk/Essen/…, das aus … kommt/mit … gefüllt ist/…	
I'm allergic to …	Ich bin allergisch gegen …	

Food (Essen)

vegetables	das Gemüse	**fruit**	das Obst
bell pepper	die Paprika	**apple**	der Apfel
carrot	die Karotte, die Möhre	**banana**	die Banane
		lemon	die Zitrone
cucumber	die Gurke	**orange**	die Orange
olive	die Olive	**strawberry,** *pl* **strawberries**	die Erdbeere
potato, *pl* **potatoes**	die Kartoffel		
tomato, *pl* **tomatoes**	die Tomate		

Meals (Mahlzeiten, fertige Gerichte)

fish and chips	Fisch mit Pommes	**biscuit**	der Keks
		bread	das Brot
meat	das Fleisch	**cake**	der Kuchen
pasta with tomato sauce	Nudeln mit Tomatensauce	**cereal**	die Frühstücks-flocken *(Pl.)*
salad	der Salat *(zubereitet)*	**cheese**	der Käse
		yoghurt	der Joghurt
soup	die Suppe		
vegetable curry	das Gemüse-curry		

Drinks (Getränke)

juice	der Saft	**water**	das Wasser
tea	der Tee	**milk**	die Milch

Describing food (Essen beschreiben)

sweet süß • **spicy** würzig, scharf • **salty** salzig • **hot** 1. heiß 2. sehr scharf • **cold** kalt • **delicious** köstlich • **yummy** lecker

8 Let's celebrate!

Let's celebrate.

I hope the weather will be good.

Maybe the other students won't like it (the dance show).

I'm worried about ...

Don't worry.

Celebrations and parties:
decoration
food
buffet
show
party, *pl* parties

I hope it won't rain tomorrow.

Will there be enough parents to help?

I'll send it (the email) right now.

It'll be sunny and warm.

If it rains, the decorations will be ruined.

How will Mr Chan like my Jollof rice?

If your Jollof rice is too spicy for Mr Chan, he can eat your puff-puffs.

→ My Words, pp. 106–107

1 Don't worry – let's celebrate!

83 Listen to and read the dialogues on page 94.
Who is worried about what? Write in your exercise book.

… is/are worried about …

the dance show • the food • the weather

2 Perfect weather for a party?

a 84 Read the weather words in the box. What's good party weather for Jill? Listen and draw smileys: ☺ perfect ☺ OK ☹ bad

☐ sunny and hot

☐ rainy and cold

☐ sunny and windy

☐ sunny and warm

Weather words

sunny
rainy
windy
cloudy
cold
cool
warm
hot

Talking about the weather:
sunny
windy
rainy
cloudy
cold
cool
warm
hot

perfect
OK
bad

b What do you think? Talk to a partner.

It's perfect for a party when it's hot and sunny. What do you think?

I don't like it when it's hot. I think it's perfect when it's warm.

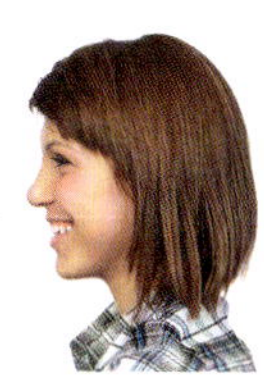

It's perfect for a party when it's hot and sunny.

TIP: Change the green words in the dialogue.

3 A happy ending for the party?

Complete the sentences with the words in the box.

dance show • email • parents • party • weather

outside ↔ inside

1 If Mo's group practises enough, the ____________ will be great.

2 If Jill sends the ________ now, there will be enough __________ at the party.

3 If the __________ is good, the ________ will be outside.

→ My Words, pp. 106–107

1 The *will*-future: positive and negative statements

a Read the boxes. Then complete the sentences about the *will*-future.

I'll You'll He/She/It'll (= will) We'll You'll They'll	be worried. celebrate. come.

I You He/She/It We You They	won't (= will not)	be worried. celebrate. come.

You form the will-future with will/won't and the infinitive of the verb:
It'll be sunny and warm tomorrow.
I hope it won't rain.
Maybe there won't be enough parents.

You use the *will*-future to say what you think or know about the future. There are often signal words like tomorrow, next week, …

⚠ Don't use the *will*-future to talk about plans for the future. For plans use the *going to*-future. → Module 6, p. 70 (*going to*-future)

going to-future • 'll • ~~will~~ • *will*-future • won't

1 Use will ________ or ________ and the infinitive in positive sentences.
2 Use ________ and the infinitive in negative sentences.
3 Use the ________ to say what you think about the future.
4 Use the ________ to say what you plan for the future.

b Read page 94 again and complete the sentences. Then match the sentences to the people.

1 Mo: A People ________ the show.
2 Olga: B Maybe the other students ________ it.
3 Yero: C I hope it ________ tomorrow.

c Complete the sentences with *'ll (will)* or *won't*.

1 There'll ________ be lots of food for the buffet, but there ________ be enough cold drinks.
2 It ________ be very hot and sunny tomorrow. I'm sure it ________ rain.
3 People ________ just sit and eat. They ________ dance a lot too.
4 People ________ love the decorations, but they ________ clean up after the party.

2 The *will*-future: questions and short answers

Read the boxes. Then match the questions to the short answers.

Will	I you he/she/it we you they	be there? come? like it?

Yes,	I/you he/she/it we/you/they	will.
No,	I/you he/she/it we/you/they	won't.

1 Will it rain on the day of the school party?
2 Will Mr Chan eat more Jollof rice?
3 Will Jill write the email to the parents?
4 Will the parents bring more food?

A No, he won't.
B Yes, they will.
C No, it won't.
D Yes, she will.

3 The *will*-future: questions with question words

a Read the boxes. Then write the question words in your language. Check in a dictionary.

Who will come to the party tomorrow?
Where will it be?
What will we do?
When will it be?

English	German	Your language
who?	wer?	___
what?	was?	___
where?	wo?	___
when?	wann?	___
why?	warum?	___

b Read the answers. Then complete the questions with the right question words.

What • When • Where • Who

1 ______ will the party start? – I think it'll start at seven o'clock.
2 ______ will we celebrate? – We'll celebrate at the youth club.
3 ______ will you make for the buffet? – I'll make a fruit salad.
4 ______ will be there? – Our friends and classmates will be there.

c Write the questions and complete the answers.

1 ~~When~~ | be home | you | will | ?
When ______ – I think I'll be home at ______

2 do | What | you | will | ?
______ – Maybe I'll ______

4 The *will*-future: making wishes and predictions

a Read the blue boxes. Then complete the sentences with phrases from the green box and *will* or *won't*.

I'm sure the weather will/won't be good.
I hope they'll/won't bring a cake.
Maybe there will/won't be a disco.
I think it will rain.
I **don't** think it **will** rain.

With the *will*-future you can say what you think or know about the future (predictions) or what you hope for the future (wishes).
You often use phrases like
I think, I hope, Maybe, I'm sure.
⚠ When you make **negative sentences with *I think***, you usually say *I don't think … will …*

1 *I'm sure* ________ we ________ have school tomorrow.
2 ________ I ________ get a good mark in the English test.
3 ________ it ________ rain today.
4 ________ my cousin ________ visit me at the weekend.

I hope • I'm sure • Maybe • I think • I don't think

b Compare your sentences with a partner.

c How will they live in ten years? Read the speech bubbles. Number the pictures (1–3).

1 Maybe I won't be a famous footballer. But I hope I'll be a very good football player.

2 I'm sure I'll be a dancer. Maybe I'll have a dance school.

3 I don't think I'll live in Russia. Maybe I'll live in the US. I hope I'll work at a theatre.

d What will you do or where will you be in ten years?
Write three sentences or more. Look up more words in a dictionary.

I'm sure I hope Maybe	I'll I won't	be have live in …	a football player • a teacher • a famous person • … a family • children • a shop • a cafe • … England • Germany • Guinea • Syria • … …
I (don't) think	I'll		

I'm sure I won't be a teacher. But maybe I'll work with children …

e Compare your sentences with a partner.

5 Conditional sentences (type 1)

a Read the box. Then match the sentence parts.
Mark the simple present and the *will*-future or *can*.

If-clause (condition)	**Main clause (result)**
If it rains,	we will celebrate inside.
If the weather is good,	we will celebrate outside.
If you like chocolate,	you will like my muffins.
If you don't like meat,	you can have a sandwich.

With conditional 1 sentences you say that something can or will happen in the present or future under a certain condition.
You use the simple present in the *if*-clause and the *will*-future in the main clause. In the main clause, you can also use the modal verb *can*.

1 If it rains at the party,
2 If Mo's group doesn't practise enough,
3 If Jill doesn't write the email now,
4 If the Jollof rice is too spicy for Mr Chan,
5 If you don't like salad,

A he won't like the chilli soup.
B there won't be enough parents to help.
C the dance show won't be good.
D you can bring some snacks or bread.
E the decorations will be ruined.

b Read the boxes. Complete the sentences with the right verb forms.
Be careful: The *if*-clause can be at the beginning or the end of the sentence.

1 If you like chocolate, you will like my muffins.
2 You will like my muffins if you like chocolate.

The *if*-clause can go before **(1)** or after **(2)** the main clause.
If the *if*-clause goes after the main clause, there is no comma.

1 If Mo's group practises **(practise)** enough, the show ______ **(be)** great.
2 Many students ______ **(dance)** if Mo ______ **(teach)** them the steps.
3 If Mo's group ______ **(have)** fun, people ______ **(have)** fun too.
4 People ______ **(cheer)** a lot if they ______ **(like)** the show.
5 If people ______ **(cheer)** a lot, Mo ______ **(be)** very happy.

c Write conditional sentences. The *if*-clause can go before or after the main clause.

1 if | you'll be late for school | you don't take the bus

______

2 if | we can meet at the weekend | I'll help you with maths

______

3 if | you'll get a better mark in maths | we study together

______

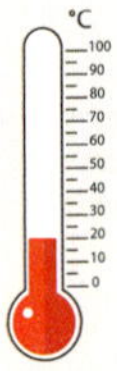

twenty degrees
(20°)

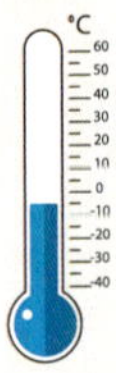

minus five degrees
(-5°)

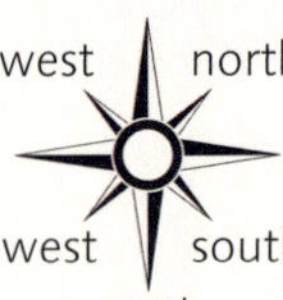

Talking about the weather:
What will the weather be like tomorrow?

weather forecast
temperature
afternoon temperatures *(pl)*
degree

1 What will the weather be like tomorrow?

a Look at the map and read.
Tick the right answer.
The weather forecast is for …

- ◯ Britain.
- ◯ Germany.
- ◯ Europe.

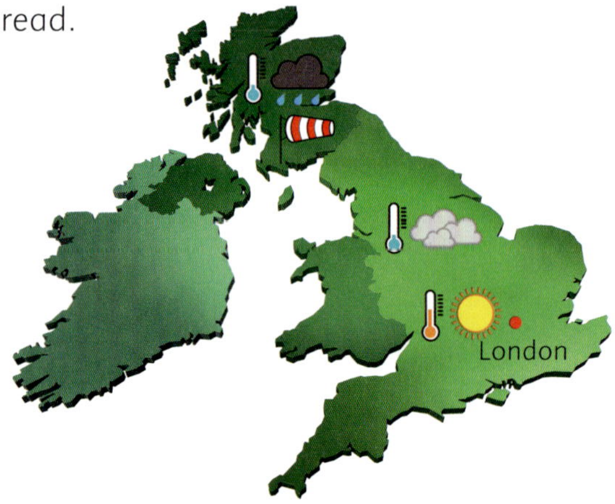

b 85 Listen to the weather forecast and complete the text.

Tomorrow it will be ________ and ________ in the north of Britain with afternoon temperatures of about ________. That's ________ for this time of the year. In the east it ________ cold too, about ________. It will be ________, but it ________ rain.
In London it will be ________ and ________, about ________.

2 There's no bad weather, only the wrong clothes!

a Look and read. Match the pictures to the weather words.

umbrella

T-shirt

gloves and hat

rain jacket

rainy and windy | cold | rainy and warm | sunny and hot

English and German

E	G
cold	kalt
sunny	sonnig
windy	windig
warm	warm

rain jacket
jacket
hat
gloves *(pl)*
umbrella

b Complete the sentences. Use the *will*-future.

a T-shirt | ~~(wear)~~ • my umbrella | (take) • (put) on | my gloves and hat • (wear) | my rain jacket

1 If it's very sunny and hot, *I'll wear* ________
2 If it's rainy and warm, ________
3 If it's very cold, ________
4 If it's rainy and windy, ________

→ My Words, pp. 106–107

c 86 Listen and check.

3 Mo's birthday party

a Read the questions. Listen and tick. 87

1 When is Mo's birthday?

- ◯ in spring ◯ in summer ◯ in autumn ◯ in winter

2 Where will Mo celebrate his birthday?

- ◯ at the school canteen ◯ at the youth club ◯ in the park

3 Will Mo ask all his classmates to come?

- ◯ Yes, all of them. ◯ No, no one. ◯ No, only Olga and Yero.

b What will happen next? Look and read. Write in your exercise book.

1. I think / I'm sure / Maybe there will be …

A There will be enough food.
B There won't be enough food.
C … (your idea)

A Mo's brother will drop the cake.
B Mo's brother won't drop the cake.
C … (your idea)

A Mo will like his aunt's present.
B Mo won't like his aunt's present.
C … (your idea)

A The music will stop.
B The music won't stop.
C … (your idea)

c Compare your ideas with a partner.

I think Mo's brother will drop the cake.

I don't agree. I'm sure he won't drop the cake.

spring
summer
autumn
winter

Positive and negative statements

⊞
I think the music **will** stop.
I'm sure the music **will** stop.
Maybe the music **will** stop.

⊟
I don't think the music **will** stop.
I'm sure the music **won't** stop.
Maybe the music **won't** stop.

What will happen next?

(to) drop sth.

→ My Words, pp. 106–107

4 Celebrations in Jill's family

a 88 Listen to three dialogues. Number the pictures (1–3).

New Year's Eve

Diwali

Christmas

b 88 Look and read. Listen again and write the things in the three lists.

presents

fireworks

flowers

candles

traditional costumes

greeting cards

traditional songs

decorations

Celebrations and parties:
present
fireworks *(pl)*
flower
candle
traditional costume
greeting card
song
decoration
New Year

Diwali: presents, ______________________

____

Christmas: ______________________

____

New Year's Eve: ______________________

____

5 Thinking about cultures

a When does your family celebrate New Year? Talk in a group.

b Collect the dates of your classmates' New Year's celebrations.

c Make a festive calendar for your classroom. Add celebrations that are important to you and your classmates.

→ My Words, pp. 106–107

6 Your favourite celebration

a Collect your ideas in the mind map. You can use words from page 102.

TIP: Do some online research if you need more information. You can look up words in an online dictionary.
→ Module 2, p. 26 (Online dictionaries and apps)

1 **My favourite celebration:** ______________________

2 When do you celebrate? ______________________

3 Who do you celebrate with? ______________________

4 How do you celebrate? ______________________

5 What do you celebrate? ______________________

b Talk to a partner about your ideas.

c Complete the text with your ideas from 6a. Copy the text in your exercise book. You can add more information.

My favourite celebration

My favourite celebration is ______________________ (1)

We celebrate it ______________________ (2)

We celebrate with ______________________ (3)

We ______________________ (4)

____

______________ celebrates ______________ (5)

____

d Present your text in class.

→ My Words, pp. 106–107

1 How to make a mind map

TIP: How to make a mind map:
1. Collect ideas for your topic – as many as you can.
2. Find word groups and umbrella words.
3. Draw your mind map on a piece of paper: Write the topic in the middle and connect the umbrella words and word groups.
4. You can use a different colour for each umbrella word and word group.
5. You can also draw pictures.

→ Look at the mind maps on pages 51, 76, 86 and 103.

a Look at the mind map and read the boxes. Tick the right answers.

A **mind map** can help you to structure your ideas. Think of a **topic**: *my favourite food, school subjects,* … Collect your ideas and write them on a piece of paper. Make **word groups** and find **umbrella words** for your word groups. Draw your mind map.

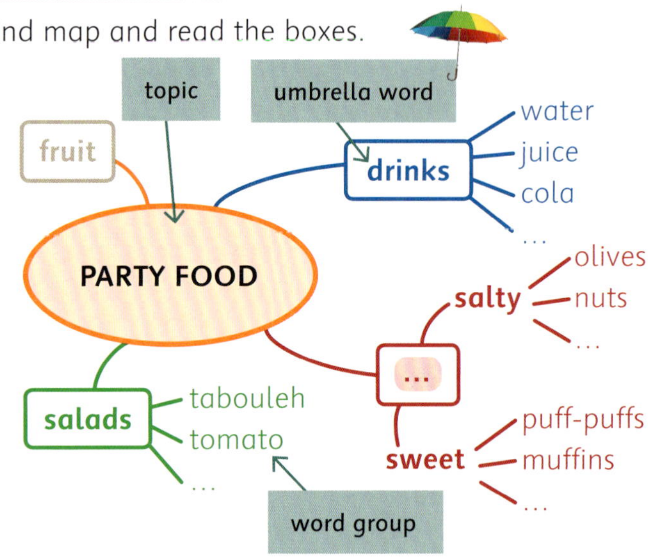

1 What's the topic of this mind map?

☐ My favourite food ☐ Party food ☐ Drinks

2 What's the missing umbrella word (…)?

☐ hot drinks ☐ sweets ☐ snacks

3 Which two words can you add to the umbrella word *salads*?

☐ fruit ☐ cake ☐ soup ☐ potato ☐ tea

TIP: You can look up more words in an online dictionary.

→ Module 2, p. 26 (Online dictionaries and apps)

b Make a mind map about your dream party. Read and write.

1. Collect ideas for the topic *My dream party*.

celebrate with all friends • listen to cool music • dance • …

2. Make word groups and write down umbrella words for your word groups. You can choose umbrella words from the box.

decorations • drinks • food • games and activities • music • place • …

3. Write the topic in the middle of the page. Write down the umbrella words and connect them to the topic.
4. Write down the word groups and connect them to the umbrella words.

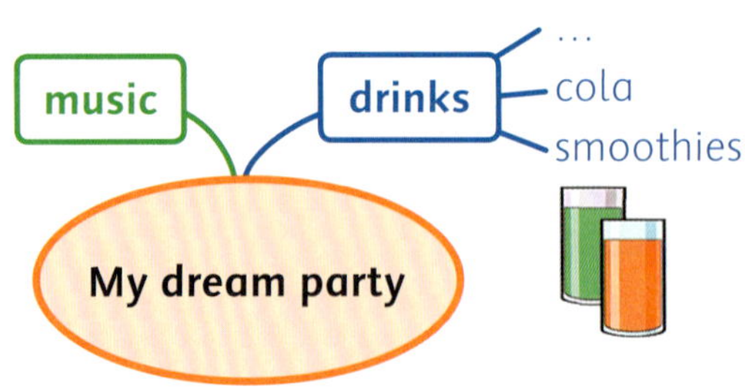

c With the help of your mind map, write a short text or give a short talk about your dream party.

My dream party takes place on the beach. All my friends are there. We're listening to cool music …

→ My Words, pp. 106–107

1 Write down the right umbrella word for each word group.

clothes • weather • vegetables

____

bell pepper, carrot, cucumber, tomato

____

T-shirt, trousers, skirt, pullover

____

sunny, cloudy, windy, rainy, hot, cold

2 89 Look and listen. Complete the text.

Tomorrow it ________ rainy and ________ in the ________ of Britain. The afternoon ________ will only be ________. In the ________ it will be warmer, about ________. It will be ________ in the morning, but ________ in the afternoon. In the ________ and south-west it ________ ________ at about ________.

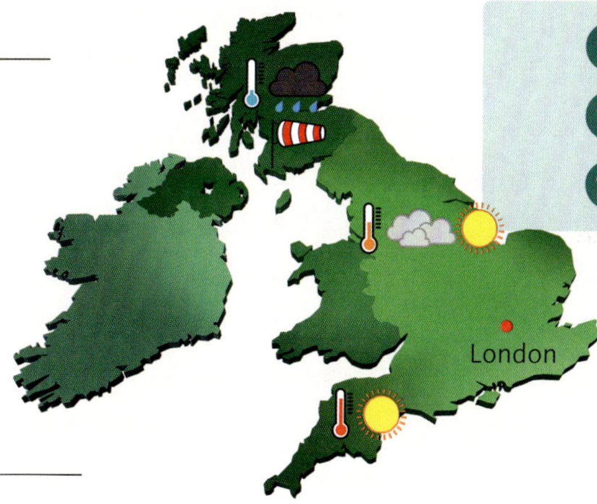

3 Complete the questions with question words.

1 ______ will our class party start? – It'll start at three o'clock.
2 ______ will we celebrate? – I think we'll celebrate in the park.
3 ______ will be there? – All our classmates will be there, I hope.
4 ______ will we do there? – I think we'll play volleyball and have a picnic.
5 ______ will we eat? – We'll have cold snacks and salads for the picnic.

4 Complete the sentences with the right verb forms.

1 If it ______ **(be)** sunny on Saturday, we ______ **(go)** to the park.
2 If we ______ **(be)** enough people, we ______ **(play)** football.
3 We ______ **(have)** a picnic if people ______ **(bring)** some food.
4 If we ______ **(not have)** enough food, we ______ **(buy)** a pizza.

English	German	My notes
I hope the weather will be good.	Ich hoffe, dass das Wetter gut wird.	
Maybe the other students won't like the dance show.	Vielleicht werden die anderen Schüler die Tanzshow nicht mögen.	
Will there be enough parents to help?	Werden genug Eltern da sein, um zu helfen?	
I'll send the email right now.	Ich schicke die Email jetzt gleich.	
How will Mr Chan like my Jollof rice?	Wie wird Herrn Chan mein Jollof-Reis schmecken?	
If it **rains**, the decorations **will be** ruined.	Wenn es regnet, wird die Dekoration kaputtgehen.	
If your Jollof rice **is** too spicy for Mr Chan, he **can** eat your puff-puffs.	Wenn dein Jollof-Reis für Herrn Chan zu scharf ist, kann er deine Puff-Puffs essen.	
Let's celebrate.	Lass(t) uns feiern.	
Celebrations and parties:	**Feiern und Partys:**	
decoration	die Dekoration	
food	das Essen	
buffet	das Büfett	
show	die Show	
party, *pl* parties	die Party, *(Pl.)* die Partys	
present	das Geschenk	
fireworks *(pl)*	das Feuerwerk; die Feuerwerkskörper *(Pl.)*	
flower	die Blume	
candle	die Kerze	
traditional costume	das traditionelle Kostüm	
greeting card	die Grußkarte	
song	das Lied	
New Year	(das) Neujahr	
(to) celebrate outside/inside	draußen/drinnen feiern	

English	German	My notes
Wishes and predictions (Wünsche und Vorhersagen)		
I think it will rain.	Ich glaube, dass es regnen wird.	
I don't think it will rain.	Ich glaube nicht, dass es regnen wird.	
I'm sure it will (won't) ...	Ich bin sicher, dass es (nicht) ...	
I hope it will (won't) ...	Ich hoffe, dass es (nicht) ...	
Maybe it will (won't) ...	Ich hoffe, dass es (nicht) ...	
(to) forget (about) sth.	etwas vergessen	
(to) drop sth.	etwas fallen lassen	
I'm worried about ... Don't worry.	Ich mache mir Sorgen über ... Mach dir keine Sorgen. / Macht euch keine Sorgen.	
What will happen next?	Was wird als nächstes passieren?	
It's perfect/OK/bad for a party when it's sunny.	Es ist perfekt/OK/schlecht für eine Party, wenn es sonnig ist.	
What will the weather be like tomorrow?	Wie wird das Wetter morgen sein?	
It'll be sunny and warm.	Es wird sonnig und warm sein.	
Talking about the weather (Über das Wetter sprechen) **cloudy** bewölkt • **cold** kalt • **cool** kühl • **hot** heiß • **rainy** regnerisch • **sunny** sonnig • **warm** warm • **windy** windig • **temperature** die Temperatur • **afternoon temperatures** die Temperaturen am Nachmittag • **degree** der Grad • **twenty degrees (20°)** zwanzig Grad • **minus five degrees (-5°)** minus fünf Grad • **(to) rain** regnen • **weather forecast** die Wettervorhersage **east** der Osten; östlich • **north** der Norden; nördlich • **south** der Süden; südlich • **west** der Westen; westlich		
spring	der Frühling	
summer	der Sommer	
autumn	der Herbst	
winter	der Winter	
Clothes (Kleidung) **gloves** *(pl)* die Handschuhe *(Pl.)* • **hat** die Mütze; der Hut • **jacket** die Jacke • **rain jacket** die Regenjacke • **umbrella** der Regenschirm; der Sonnenschirm		

infinitive	simple past	past participle	German
be [biː]	was [wɒz]	been [biːn]	sein; war; (ist) gewesen
buy [baɪ]	bought [bɔːt]	bought [bɔːt]	kaufen; kaufte; (hat) gekauft
come [kʌm]	came [keɪm]	come [kʌm]	kommen; kam; (ist) gekommen
cut [kʌt]	cut [kʌt]	cut [kʌt]	schneiden; schnitt; (hat) geschnitten
do [duː]	did [dɪd]	done [dʌn]	tun; tat; (hat) getan
drink [drɪŋk]	drank [dræŋk]	drunk [drʌŋk]	trinken; trank; (hat) getrunken
eat [iːt]	ate [et, eɪt]	eaten [ˈiːtn]	essen; aß; (hat) gegessen
forget [fəˈget]	forgot [fəˈgɒt]	forgotten [fəˈgɒtn]	vergessen; vergaß; (hat) vergessen
get [get]	got [gɒt]	got [gɒt]	bekommen; bekam; (hat) bekommen
go [gəʊ]	went [went]	gone [gɒn]	gehen; ging; (ist) gegangen
have [hæv]	had [hæd]	had [hæd]	haben; hatte; (hat) gehabt
lie [laɪ]	lay [leɪ]	lain [leɪn]	liegen; lag; (hat) gelegen
make [meɪk]	made [meɪd]	made [meɪd]	machen; machte; (hat) gemacht
meet [miːt]	met [met]	met [met]	treffen; traf; (hat) getroffen

infinitive	simple past	past participle	German
put [pʊt]	put [pʊt]	put [pʊt]	legen, stellen; legte, stellte; (hat) gelegt, (hat) gestellt
read [ri:d]	read [red]	read [red]	lesen; las; (hat) gelesen
see [si:]	saw [sɔ:]	seen [si:n]	sehen; sah; (hat) gesehen
sew [səʊ]	sewed [səʊd]	sewn [səʊn]	nähen; nähte; (hat) genäht
sit [sɪt]	sat [sæt]	sat [sæt]	sitzen; saß; (hat) gesessen
speak [spi:k]	spoke [spəʊk]	spoken ['spəʊkən]	sprechen; sprach; (hat) gesprochen
stand [stænd]	stood [stʊd]	stood [stʊd]	stehen; stand; (hat) gestanden
take [teɪk]	took [tʊk]	taken ['teɪkən]	nehmen; nahm; (hat) genommen
teach [ti:tʃ]	taught [tɔ:t]	taught [tɔ:t]	unterrichten; unterrichtete; (hat) unterrichtet
tell [tel]	told [təʊld]	told [təʊld]	erzählen, berichten; erzählte, berichtete; (hat) erzählt, (hat) berichtet
think [θɪŋk]	thought [θɔ:t]	thought [θɔ:t]	denken; dachte; (hat) gedacht
wear [weə]	wore [wɔ:]	worn [wɔ:n]	tragen; trug; (hat) getragen
win [wɪn]	won [wɒn]	won [wɒn]	gewinnen; gewann; (hat) gewonnen

English sounds

[iː]	green, he, sea
[ɑː]	ask, class, car, park
[ɔː]	or, ball, door, four, morning
[uː]	ruler, blue, too, two, you
[ɜː]	early, her, girl, work, T-shirt
[ɪ]	in, big, expensive
[e]	yes, bed, again, breakfast
[æ]	animal, apple, black, cat
[ʌ]	mum, bus, colour
[ɒ]	song, on, dog, what
[ʊ]	book, good, pullover
[ə]	again, today, a sister
[i]	happy, monkey
[eɪ]	name, eight, play, great
[aɪ]	I, time, right, my
[ɔɪ]	boy, toilet, noise
[əʊ]	old, no, road, yellow
[aʊ]	now, house
[eə]	where, pair, share, their
[ʊə]	tour

[b]	bike, table, verb
[p]	pen, paper, shop
[d]	day, window, good
[t]	ten, letter, at
[g]	go, again, bag
[k]	kitchen, car, back
[m]	man, remember, mum
[n]	no, one, ten
[ŋ]	wrong, young, uncle, thanks
[l]	like, old, small
[r]	ruler, friend, sorry
[w]	we, where, one
[j]	yes, you, uniform
[f]	family, after, laugh
[v]	very, seven, have
[s]	six, poster, yes
[z]	zoo, quiz, his, music, please
[ʃ]	she, station, English
[ʒ]	usually, revision, garage
[tʃ]	child, teacher, watch
[dʒ]	job, German, project, orange
[θ]	thing, three, bathroom, both
[ð]	the, father, with
[h]	house, who, behind

The English alphabet

A, a	[eɪ]	H, h	[eɪtʃ]	O, o	[əʊ]	V, v	[viː]
B, b	[biː]	I, i	[aɪ]	P, p	[piː]	W, w	['dʌbljuː]
C, c	[siː]	J, j	[dʒeɪ]	Q, q	[kjuː]	X, x	[eks]
D, d	[diː]	K, k	[keɪ]	R, r	[ɑː]	Y, y	[waɪ]
E, e	[iː]	L, l	[el]	S, s	[es]	Z, z	[zed]
F, f	[ef]	M, m	[em]	T, t	[tiː]		
G, g	[dʒiː]	N, n	[en]	U, u	[juː]		

English numbers

0	oh, zero [əʊ, ˈzɪəpəʊ]		
1	one [wʌn]	1st	first [fɜːst]
2	two [tuː]	2nd	second [ˈsekənd]
3	three [θriː]	3rd	third [θɜːd]
4	four [fɔː]	4th	fourth [fɔːθ]
5	five [faɪv]	5th	fifth [fɪfθ]
6	six [sɪks]	6th	sixth [sɪksθ]
7	seven [ˈsevn]	7th	seventh [ˈsevnθ]
8	eight [eɪt]	8th	eighth [eɪtθ]
9	nine [naɪn]	9th	ninth [naɪnθ]
10	ten [ten]	10th	tenth [tenθ]
11	eleven [ɪˈlevn]	11th	eleventh [ɪˈlevnθ]
12	twelve [twelv]	12th	twelfth [twelfθ]
13	thirteen [θɜːˈtiːn]	13th	thirteenth [θɜːˈtiːnθ]
14	fourteen [fɔːˈtiːn]	14th	fourteenth [fɔːˈtiːnθ]
15	fifteen [fɪfˈtiːn]	15th	fifteenth [fɪfˈtiːnθ]
16	sixteen [sɪksˈtiːn]	16th	sixteenth [sɪksˈtiːnθ]
17	seventeen [sevnˈtiːn]	17th	seventeenth [sevnˈtiːnθ]
18	eighteen [eɪˈtiːn]	18th	eighteenth [eɪˈtiːnθ]
19	nineteen [naɪnˈtiːn]	19th	nineteenth [naɪnˈtiːnθ]
20	twenty [ˈtwenti]	20th	twentieth [ˈtwentiəθ]
21	twenty-one [twentiˈwʌn]	21st	twenty-first [twentiˈfɜːst]
22	twenty-two [twentiˈtuː]	22nd	twenty-second [twentiˈsekənd]
23	twenty-three [twentiˈθriː]	23rd	twenty-third [twentiˈθɜːd]
...		...	
30	thirty [ˈθɜːti]	30th	thirtieth [ˈθɜːtiəθ]
40	forty [ˈfɔːti]	40th	fortieth [ˈfɔːtiəθ]
50	fifty [ˈfɪfti]	50th	fiftieth [ˈfɪftiəθ]
60	sixty [ˈsɪksti]	60th	sixtieth [ˈsɪkstiəθ]
70	seventy [ˈsevnti]	70th	seventieth [ˈsevntiəθ]
80	eighty [ˈeɪti]	80th	eightieth [ˈeɪtiəθ]
90	ninety [ˈnaɪnti]	90th	ninetieth [ˈnaɪntiəθ]
100	a/one hundred [ə/wʌn ˈhʌndrəd]	100th	hundredth [ˈhʌndrədθ]
101	one hundred and one	101st	hundred and first
102	one hundred and two	102nd	hundred and second
...		...	

Classroom English

You and your teacher	Du und dein Lehrer/deine Lehrerin
Good morning, Mr/Mrs …	Guten Morgen, Herr/Frau …
Good afternoon, Mr/Mrs …	Guten Tag, Herr/Frau …
Can I open/close the window, please?	Kann ich bitte das Fenster öffnen/zumachen?
Can I go to the toilet, please?	Kann ich bitte zur Toilette gehen?
Goodbye. See you tomorrow.	Auf Wiedersehen. Bis morgen.
Homework and exercises	**Hausaufgaben und Übungen**
I don't understand this exercise.	Ich verstehe die Übung nicht.
Sorry, I don't know.	Es tut mir leid, das weiß ich nicht.
What's for homework?	Was haben wir als Hausaufgabe auf?
Can I work with Nour?	Kann ich mit Nour arbeiten?
You need help	**Du brauchst Hilfe**
Can you help me, please?	Können Sie mir bitte helfen?
What's … in English/German?	Was heißt … auf Englisch/Deutsch?
Can I say it in German?	Kann ich das auf Deutsch sagen?
Can you say/play that again, please?	Können Sie das bitte noch einmal sagen/abspielen?
What your teacher says	**Was dein Lehrer/deine Lehrerin sagt**
Listen, please.	Hört bitte zu.
Quiet, please.	Ruhe bitte.
Open your books at page 24, please.	Schlagt bitte Seite 24 auf.
Look at picture A.	Seht euch Bild A an.
Do exercise 5 for homework, please.	Macht bitte Übung 5 als Hausaufgabe.
Where's your book/exercise book?	Wo ist dein Buch/Übungsheft?
That's very good.	Das ist sehr gut.
Correct the mistakes.	Korrigiert die Fehler.
Make a poster about …	Macht ein Poster zum Thema …
That's all for today. You can go.	Das ist alles für heute. Ihr könnt gehen.